"This is a transformative work. The book is important for the medical profession, caregivers, and anyone wishing to support others."

— John Caskey, MD, Santa Fe, New Mexico

"I think it's the best book I ever read. It does a superb job of weaving together things which had heretofore been seen as disparate … I want to see this out there as soon as possible. I think it's that important."

— Bonnie Long, cancer survivor and near-death experiencer, Seattle, Washington

"It is stunning! Engaged me from start to finish! There was not a single chapter that I did not relish … I particularly admired your ability to write about complex and fundamental truths with such engaging simplicity. I loved the personal stories … it was like reading a novel and looking forward to what would happen to the characters."

— Gordon Allan, founder, The Aletheia Group, Toronto, Canada

"Great book! Catch this easy read about healing, transformation, creation, death, and beyond death. Jim Macartney tells of his and numerous others' experiences to evidence his case."

— Leo Kim, PhD, author of *Healing the Rift: Bridging the Gap Between Science and Spirituality*

"*Crisis to Creation* provides dramatic evidence of the power of choice to heal the soul, transform tragedy into blessings, and take people from crisis into creation. One sees just how miraculously "can" triumphs over "can't." Whether you have suffered tragedy or not, this book will transform you."

— Yolaine M. Stout, president, American Center for the Integration of Spiritually Transformative Experiences, San Diego, California

"In this well-written book regarding post-traumatic growth, James Macartney synthesizes both science and spirituality to explore how we as individuals can emerge from the depths of crisis and chaos in order to reach an even more meaningful level of existence and a higher understanding of the human condition."

— Belle Harrell, PhD, teacher, Columbus, Georgia

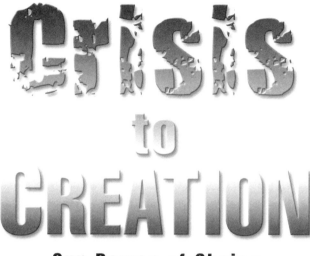

Crisis to CREATION

Our Power of Choice

JAMES W. MACARTNEY

BOOK PUBLISHERS NETWORK

Book Publishers Network
PO Box 2256
Bothell, WA 98041
Ph 425-483-3040

Printed in the United States of America.

LCCN: 2010903460
ISBN10: 1-935359-32-0
ISBN13: 978-1-935359-32-6

Cover Design: Laura Zugzda
Author Photo: Elke Macartney
Interior Layout: Mi Ae Lipe, What Now Design
Illustrations: Alan Bagshaw, Apogee Communications

Author's note: Only first names are used in those cases where I wish to protect the identity of the individual. The one exception is the name of Dr. Sylvia Sanders, which is a pseudonym.

This book is dedicated to each and every one of us,
whenever we choose to be the creative force in our own life.

Contents

Acknowledgments ix

Introduction xi

CHAPTER 1   Pushed Off the Edge 1

CHAPTER 2   Caught in Collapsing Realities 11

CHAPTER 3   When Chaos Brings Transformation 29

CHAPTER 4   The Creation Cycle 45

CHAPTER 5   Who Is the Chooser? 59

CHAPTER 6   Supporting Others 83

CHAPTER 7   Some Just Forget to Die 99

CHAPTER 8   How We Institutionalize Disability 121

CHAPTER 9   Empowered Helping Systems 135

CHAPTER 10   A Culture of Crisis 153

CHAPTER 11   Beyond the Edge of Science 173

CHAPTER 12   Beyond the Edge of Life 191

Epilogue 205

Bibliography 207

Permissions 211

Acknowledgments

This book is a co-creation with all those who have imprinted themselves on my life by their presence and inspiration. For each of you who have touched my life, I am grateful for what you have taught me, and for the possibilities of fulfillment you daily model to everyone around you.

While in graduate school I met a young woman who had just been diagnosed with uterine cancer, and observed how she came to fully face her life from a place of utter honesty. I've had the fortunate opportunity to closely follow this woman's journey these many years, for she has since birthed my two children. In turn, she has walked alongside a husband who almost died, incurred brain and heart damage, had open-heart surgery, and was determined disabled not once, but twice. To the love of my life, Elke, I walk hand in hand with you to ever new, ever more conscious and fulfilling creations on this planet of opportunity.

To my sons Ryan and Eron, miracles in themselves, who both are etching their own creations into the fabric of time. To my sister Anne Brooks and my sister-in-law Laurie Macartney, who both choose to thrive and reach out to serve others in the wake of their own journeys with breast cancer.

To my friend and mentor, Bob Branscom, who helped me take the leap from thinking to being, from striving to letting go to my own inner source of creativity and well-being.

To the physicians who are helping to keep me on the planet. My gratitude goes to Dr. David Dillard, who challenged me to find my own limits and therefore transcend them, and to Dr. David Gartman, who demonstrated the power of the Creation Cycle by letting go to a surgical solution when none existed, thereby saving my life. To Jahuda Sepkuty, MD, and Jonathon

Lowy, MD, for their rare capacity to set aside their considerable expertise—and listen without judgment.

To Lee Blackstock and all the staff at Favorite Associates for their unwavering support; Lee Carroll and Kim Sharp-Clark, who sparked my new career path by inviting me to speak at their respective conferences; Darci Olsen and Potlatch pool—where after being diagnosed with congestive heart failure, I went from spluttering a half length to several years later swimming a half mile.

To those who gave encouragement and support along the road of my life—leading me to ever higher levels of understanding that continue to grow daily. These include Max Eckenberg, who singlehandedly created a nationally recognized High Adventure program I was fortunate enough to help lead; Jane Billinghurst, an editor who years ago literally tore my book apart, telling me to drop the academic tone and tell people's stories—especially my own; Bill Malcomson, PhD, and Ken Kuhn, PhD, for their kind encouragement and review of the text; and so many more who taught and inspired me to reach further than I thought possible.

Introduction

We live in complex and confusing times. From daily irritations to major traumas, personal tragedy to cultural upheavals, we constantly adjust our thoughts and actions to stay in balance and secure our safety in order to move ahead in life—hopefully.

Of course, "moving ahead" means something very different for each of us, from rising through the corporate boardroom to expanding our understanding of our place in the cosmos to living long enough to see a grandchild born or a dream unfold. We sometimes wander blindly, following well-worn paths trod by our grandfathers and grandmothers—in the hope that they will lead us to a more solid sense of what constitutes fulfillment and well-being.

Much of the modern world is engaged in defense of hard-earned goods, livelihoods, and cherished beliefs about who and what we are. We expend considerable personal and national treasure to keep them protected from known and unknown threats.

But what we've built over a lifetime or many generations can be snuffed out in an instant. People riding the wave of success may, in a brief twist of a tornado snout or highway roundabout, spin out of control to find themselves helpless in the face of overwhelming forces that shatter all they hold dear.

To be clear: Bookstores everywhere are full of personal growth and self-help guides, many of them extolling techniques such as positive thinking, affirmation, and other popular change strategies. Often these are oriented to helping us fix some problem in our lives or to creating the ideal circumstances we wish to have surrounding us.

While these can be very helpful, this book isn't one of them.

Instead, it offers guideposts to another perhaps more deeply human path: Within any crisis, the seeds of renewal await our own personal choice of attitude and action. *Crisis to Creation* both draws upon and adds to what's already known about the transformational dynamics often seen in what's been termed "post-traumatic growth" (PTG). Above all, it points to how individuals' attitudes become fundamental in shaping and sustaining a quality life regardless of circumstances.

You will read about those who have pioneered this path. The people I call *choice makers* gift us with insights and tools to help each one of us along our own increasingly uncertain journey to the future. They demonstrate a future created through the power of their own thoughts and actions.

The concepts and processes laid forth in this book emerged from my personal life and my work over the last twenty years counseling youth, adults, and families in crisis or recovery. In 1988, I began a focused search for people who transformed their lives in the wake of deep crisis. The Creation Cycle described in Chapter 4 gradually revealed itself from the distinct patterns seen in those who either remained scarred and limited by crisis or grew and flourished.

Underlying any new creation lies choice: Our ability to choose is constrained to what we perceive. The Circle of Perception in Chapter 5 casts its net around the whole of reality as we experience it in any moment. The contents within the net contain all the experiences, feelings, emotions, meanings, values, and beliefs within the range of our awareness. Choose a new perception—and the net closes upon a fresh new catch of reality.

Neither the Circle of Perception nor the Creation Cycle requires theory or authority for validation; they naturally reveal themselves in direct experience. This book is designed to open readers to the possibility for becoming the creative force in their own lives and to show ways of putting one's creative energy into action.

A word about courage. Many readers might think that the remarkable stories written in this book point to people who are extra courageous, gifted somehow to reach beyond the ordinary. When I relate stories of choice makers to those trapped in irresolvable crisis, they often state, "I can see how *they* might succeed, but they had something I don't have. And they don't have *my* problem."

One way to remain disabled is to see others as somehow special, so it justifies remaining trapped and limited. To counter this misperception, I want to insert a note from my book designer after her initial review of the manuscript:

> *I cannot tell you how many times people thought I was brave and courageous to leave my profoundly unhappy married life to start anew in an unfamiliar city across the country, or to survive a childhood filled with physical and emotional abuse.*
>
> *The truth is that it had nothing to do with courage at all. It was something I simply had to do, because the alternative was to either commit suicide or live the rest of my life numb and bitter with resentment. When faced with such ultimate choices, we simply need to choose the beginning of the rest of our lives, and live well. To think of such people as courageous, while it is well-intentioned by well-meaning others, romanticizes and sentimentalizes a decidedly unromantic situation.*

We are *all* choice makers. This book opens the possibility for each of us to create a life of richness without having to be pushed to the extremes of crisis. Or, if we are already trapped within its jaws, to know that the immense power of choice always resides within us.

Jim Macartney
La Conner, Washington, February 2010

Chapter 1
Pushed Off the Edge

What doesn't kill us makes us stronger. Right?

— Author —

On a moonless night in May of 1997, I awoke to a firefighter in full regalia tromping through my bedroom. Drowsily, I wondered for a moment how he got there... and why did my clock say it was 3:30 AM? A second firefighter walked in the door, also dressed as if he was going to a fire. From my days working as a firefighter while in college, I knew how cumbersome and sweaty fire gear could be, especially indoors.

My pondering trailed off as I dreamily drifted into peace-filled sleep.

Moments later, I awoke to another firefighter busily clipping a probe on my index finger. More alert now, I sat up and took in the scene: Four firefighters and my wife, all regarding me intently—she, fully clothed, on the bed next to me, and they in their heavy gear, surrounding the bed. Everybody looked markedly relieved for some reason.

The scene made absolutely no sense to me in my state of bliss and peace. If I could have but rid myself of this hallucination of firefighters, I'd have liked nothing better than to have pulled my wife under the sheets and drifted back into dreamland.

Waking Up, Rudely

My reverie, however, was shattered again by these intruders. Against my protestations of feeling quite better than better, they laid more gear on the bed, opened their black medical kits scarred by many years of use, and methodically began to check my vitals. Feeling overwhelmed by all the commotion, I focused on the firefighter kneeling by my side and, as firmly as I could, ordered him to repack his gear and cease the poking and prodding! My protests ignored, I felt wires sliding over my arm and a pinch as he reattached the probe to my finger.

Agitated, I detached their instruments. The firefighter patiently reattached the probes. I detached them. Then they more forcefully reattached them, one firefighter commanding, "You will leave these on!"

I scrunched my forehead quizzically in my wife's direction, imploring her help.

"Maybe it would be a good idea if you let them to do their job, Honey," she said. "Just humor them."

After more poking and prodding, the firefighter announced we were bound for the hospital. But while I acceded to the general plan—my Benedict Arnold of a wife having joined their ranks—I refused to be strapped on a stretcher and manhandled down the narrow stairway of our house as if I were a corpse. Still in pajamas, I allowed myself to be silently escorted outside to flashing lights of an aid car idling in our driveway.

En route to the hospital, I became aware that my overriding sense of peace and well-being masked something else: the taste of blood. Oozing from the side of my tongue, now buzzing and burning, salty warm wetness mingled with the buzzing as my mouth twisted into intense pain.

It was as if I'd bitten my tongue. Hard.

Even more confused now, I wondered how my tongue could be buzzing and bleeding when my mind remained immersed in this wonderful sea of peace. By the time we reached the small community hospital near my home, my tongue felt like an oversized ringing alarm clock stuffed into my mouth.

The Sentence—Lingering Disability

Once at the hospital, doctors poked and prodded some more and then sent me off for test after test. Finally, they settled on a tentative diagnosis of brain and heart damage resulting from a catastrophic seizure.

The aftermath: I was unable to drive, my memory processing was impaired, and my emotions remained exquisitely sensitive to stimulus. Noise, vibration, even two people talking at once overwhelmed me. Going to a busy place like a shopping mall was much like stepping inside a rock crusher.

After months of exhaustive neurological testing, the teams of doctors and independent medical examiners determined I would be incapable of working again—ironically, as a vocational rehabilitation specialist. My neurologist told me flatly that adult brains with damage similar to mine do not heal.

Suddenly facing lingering disability, just like so many of my clients, I sank into a hopeless world of confusion and limitation.

Yet more than a decade later, I find myself traveling, writing, lecturing, and being a fairly successful dad. True, both of my sons have taken to patting me on my head sympathetically when I seem clueless about what's going on in their lives. But it's clear even to them that I've reached a level of functioning not remotely anticipated when the doctors told me my condition would not change.

In fact, today I'm more engaged and fulfilled than during the years I worked as a mountain climbing guide or led wilderness search-and-rescue teams as a vigorous young adult.

So what happened? How have I managed to achieve and sustain a higher quality of life, even when many of the problems that swamped my life back in 1997 remain unvanquished?

Flashback to "Limbo"

Once I'd been placed on long-term disability, all treatment efforts ceased since, after all, *adult brains don't heal.* Saddled by a limited memory that measured in the bottom 5 percent of the adult population and unable to perform more than one simple task at a time, my "normal" life, as I knew it, ground to a halt. I lost my identity and purpose, had no ability to support my family, and was regarded as permanently damaged, both mentally and physically. Treatments and testing ceased.

As the months wore on, I couldn't surmount my own limited perspective—a constant replay of My Life Before the Seizure versus My Life After the Seizure. Truth to tell, the perspective from which I viewed my life hadn't really changed—I was still a rehabilitation professional, just one on medical leave, dependent on others to keep my life in order because I was "totally disabled."

I was unable to envision any possibility of fitting back into a competitive job market or any way to challenge my disability, even though I had many years of experience in helping others overcome their disabilities and losses.

Without a change in perspective, I couldn't see the benefit of taking *any* action, for I was locked into a world of forgetfulness where even major events slipped through my memory banks like water through a sieve.

I remained a "disabled person" for several years, unable to return to the world I knew or to envision a new one until one day came a wakeup call.

Just Coincidence?

For many years I'd been extremely interested in the edges of consciousness and had studied how human awareness itself seems to evolve. About two years after my disability, I received a phone call out of the blue, asking if, six months down the road, I would give two lectures on the topic to educators, one in Chicago and the other in Los Angeles.

Impossible. Absurd really. I could barely tolerate being in the same room with two or more people conversing at once or even remember how to find my way around my own tiny town, much less keep a string of words and thoughts in mind while standing in front of a group. The merest distraction or question from an audience member would surely obliterate whatever train of thought I might have left.

I politely said, "No, thank you."

Sinking back into my grayness, I watched my life pass by like a ship drifting aimlessly, kept afloat by disability payments but not sailing anywhere. A few days after the call, the truth struck me full force: *I was merely surviving—I was not really living at all.* I asked myself two questions. Number One: Am I willing to settle for this gray life in this box of permanent disability and, if I'm lucky, survive safely without too much more trauma until the day I die? Number Two: If I was able, what would I really want to do?

I immediately phoned the event sponsor and said "Yes!"

Shift Point

The conferences were six full months away. Somehow, I told myself, I can find a way to prepare and deliver a couple of simple lectures. My life swung into action, fueled and focused by my newfound desires, which fanned the embers of residual abilities to think and act.

I studied the latest research. I wrote daily. I created a series of PowerPoint slides to carve a visual pathway through the speech that would help keep my thoughts on track, and I prepared detailed written notes for every thirty-second increment of the presentation. This way, if I was interrupted or otherwise lost my place, I could just skip to the next piece of the talk without any apparent disruption for the audience.

Those two lectures comprised my first struggling steps back into professional life. What stands out to me, however, is what happened during the preparation period. After about four months of toil on the lecture material, I noticed an amazing thing: My memory and my ability to multitask without a meltdown had improved markedly!

Perhaps it was just coincidence. But clearly, it was only after I committed to something I wanted, even as it lay beyond what was possible—maybe *because* it demanded something new from me, to step beyond what I thought possible—that I began noticing my physical and mental abilities improving. What's more, my physical recovery seemed to unfold in response to my focused attention, and *intention*. It followed as a side effect from an internal shift within me to re-engage my life with the abilities I already possessed, however limited they seemed.

Somehow I'd shifted, almost stumbled, onto a simple and powerful tool this book terms the "Creation Cycle"—transformational dynamics I had now and again glimpsed in the recovery phase of my clients' lives, but through a glass darkly. When my own life underwent catastrophic challenges, with no established guideposts to light the way, I found myself reinventing the cycle the hard way, so to speak.

Flash Forward to This Book

Many people experience outcomes similar to mine—many much more powerful—after falling off the edge of life into the depths of crises of all types. More than sixty people I interviewed who transformed their lives subsequent to crisis, and some drawn from the many hundreds of clients I worked with professionally, all exhibited a fascinating pattern: They made a fundamental change in how they approached the obstacles in their lives and the choices they made. Fascinating and surprising similarities can be seen in how they viewed—often only in retrospect—the power of crisis as a transformative agent.

Each one emerged from a state of personal crisis and chaos to engage the full Creation Cycle highlighted in these pages.

These individuals were able to transform their loss or disability into an increased quality and deeper appreciation of life, some even as they physically remained maimed or even declined toward certain death. They illuminate a path for all of us to fully re-engage our lives ... today ... now ... regardless of the circumstances that may seem to entrap us.

Although their insights often seem to resonate with the deep wisdom traditions of the world's great faiths and philosophies, this needn't be the principal lesson their stories impart. In straightforward, practical terms, their paths disclose a vital developmental pattern that merits more systematic exploration and support.

To Promote Post-Traumatic Growth

Indeed, their splendid stories illuminate a process that has been understudied and underreported by researchers and observers until recently, as evidenced by the slim literature of "post-traumatic growth" (PTG). Strikingly, post-traumatic growth can ensue in even the most medically hopeless cases and has applications in any kind of upheaval. University of North Carolina psychologists Lawrence Calhoun and Richard Tedeschi coined the term in the 1990s based on their research findings that some people actually flourish in disaster's wake.

PTG researchers see some individuals, in the wake of severe stress, arriving at a deepened sense of connection to others, higher appreciation of life, and increased spiritual development. New interests and priorities emerge. Increasingly, researchers are focusing attention on human resilience and growth as an outgrowth to stress and crisis.

Tools to promote these outcomes have immediate application. For example, the news today reports epidemic rates of post-traumatic stress disorder (PTSD) among war veterans returning from

Iraq and Afghanistan, but we've paid little attention to the potential for long-term growth from their ordeals. Retrospective studies of Vietnam prisoners of war in the 1980s, for instance, show that while their horrendous experiences as POWs were indeed traumatic, many came to perceive them as ultimately beneficial.

Generally speaking, however, our helping institutions have scarcely recognized, much less supported, ways to promote PTG.

That could change. It's my hope that the growing attention will begin to fill the gap between what many have experienced on a self-discovered "creation track" and the juiceless rehabilitation scenarios found in many an institutional-disability mindset.

Big Questions

What does it take to emerge from crisis stronger and more engaged in life than before? When a problem becomes more than a bump in the road and threatens an individual's identity or survival, *can* we predict who will most likely return to a productive and fulfilling life?

Look carefully at the following examples of people in crisis. Care to hazard a guess as to who rebounded to enjoy and play again—even if his or her problem was not fixed? Who stayed mired in disability or confusion or dragged along hobbled by the scars of the past?

- Dr. Sanders, a surgeon who had her leg amputated, was unable to stand long enough on her prosthetic leg to perform surgery. She was forced to go on disability.

- Vivienne, a highly respected teacher, developed breast cancer and endured a double mastectomy without pain medication due to allergic reactions.

- Roger, a machinist near retirement, had intractable pain from shoulder and back injuries that caused him to suffer from deep depression and loneliness.

- Jeff, a high school football player who broke his neck, became an instant quadriplegic.

- Joan, a nurse who suffered brain damage in a small plane crash that killed her beloved husband, could not grasp either his death or her own catastrophic disability.

- Evy, director of intensive care and coronary care, was diagnosed with terminal Lou Gehrig's Disease (ALS), an incurable neurological disease, and given a year to live.

- Wayne, a marine mechanic, was told to put his affairs in order by his doctors since he was losing the battle with leukemia.

- Gary, a physicist, suffered from undiagnosed problems for years. After multiple surgeries, he was finally diagnosed with multiple sclerosis and given two years to live.

It's not possible to predict the outcomes of their stories, is it?

In the following chapters, we'll see which of these individuals, like me, did eventually regain purpose and quality of life. From closely examining their stories, we can winnow out the patterns that distinguished those who thrived from those who did not—and perhaps use them as guides for living more fully without the trauma.

Chapter 2
Caught in Collapsing Realities

There is nothing either good or bad,
but thinking makes it so.

— Shakespeare —

We all share the trauma and drama of loss and change. Any untoward event in our lives immediately focuses our attention on resolving the problem and getting back to normal. Our love suddenly leaves, or we lose a job or a house. The hole in our heart may be assuaged with a new love or a new house, and eventually we find ourselves back in the normal flow of daily life.

In retrospect our crisis seems just a bump in the road. We're caught up in our routine again, the pain forgotten, thank God! And yet…it's unlikely we've gained any new insight or growth from the experience.

But what happens when we're blocked from returning to our "normal"? Faced with no direction, no purpose, or a shattered past, how do we move on?

There's Defeat—or Magic—in Chaos

When crisis collapses the structure of our lives, we don't go gently into the chaos of uncertainty that must follow. We desperately want a world with familiar boundaries. In fact, our very human minds will latch onto any shred of meaning to organize our world so that we know how to act and react.

Because it's so difficult to tolerate the ambiguity and open-endedness of leaving behind the world we know, we cannot see any possible end to it nor anticipate any gift of newness coming from it.

Without exception, everyone I interviewed for this book at some point faced letting go of a reality no longer tenable, with nothing to take its place. Take a careful look at how crisis brought the following three individuals—Dr. Sanders, Vivienne, and Roger—to the threshold of personal chaos and how they responded.

Dr. Sanders

Sylvia Sanders was one who struggled to redefine herself and her professional work to accommodate what she saw as a permanent handicap barring her from returning to work as a surgeon.

After treating thousands of patients with debilitating injuries, Dr. Sanders herself suffered one in a skiing accident. Her leg had to be amputated below the knee. At first, she actively participated in her own rehabilitation, spending long hours researching the best treatment practices.

But here she was in her mid-50s, unable to stand and practice surgery. How to take hold of her life? Dr. Sanders felt her career was dead-ended, assuring me: "I'm too old to start over." Retraining in another specialty and going through another residency seemed too daunting to her. Doomed to a life of disability, she saw no way to fix her world.

She was staring into the abyss...

Vivienne

After being chosen Teacher of the Year in her school district, Vivienne stood at the pinnacle of her career. But when she was forty-six, doctors found several four-centimeter lumps in her breast. The news left her shocked and numb.

She confided:

When the doctors came to inform me of the need for breast surgery, I still remember a beautiful scene. They all moved in around me very close, surrounding me, all touching me as they informed me the tumor was aggressive. All these men, so detached, so scientific, all touching me.

It hit me like a sledgehammer. Bam! My life was in danger. Then they all slowly moved back like in a dance, and explained the options to me, giving me the emotional space to be with the information.

Pondering her future, Vivienne's insides tied into knots of confusion and fear. What was she going to do?

Roger

Now in his late 50s, Roger had been a machinist his whole life, beginning in his teens and advancing easily to managing and running a machine shop. He was well-liked and gregarious, the kind of guy you could trust, kind and gentle, the "salt of the earth." His thick hands and forearms showed his years of work, although, since his injury, his broad shoulders and heavyset frame had settled, his chest resting upon a spreading paunch.

Several years before, a sudden slip resulted in a debilitating back, hip, and shoulder injury that had not healed properly. Unlike many people stuck in his situation who seek safety by pushing for a disability pension or early retirement, Roger somehow found a new way to continue working in his field.

Steady and dependable, he thought he could put his lingering depression behind him and climb back into life. Time would tell.

Roger found a job sharpening the steel bits used by machinists, and for a short time he felt he was returning to a productive and stable life. But his intractable pain was compounded by the side effects of pain medication, and his foggy mind limited his ability to function on the job.

Gradually the medication pulled him down into a lingering, black depression. His periodic reference to wanting to "end it all" prompted his doctor to provide antidepressants and prescribe intervention by rehabilitation specialists.

Roger felt himself sinking into a dark void...

The Rest of Their Stories

Dr. Sanders, Vivienne, and Roger had each reached a point of painful personal reckoning: How to cope with the utter collapse of the world each had known? If you think that Dr. Sanders's education and professional background or Vivienne's popularity with her peers and students or Roger's obvious management skills and "salt-of-the-earth" groundedness could predict their ultimately surpassing their limitations to build new, fulfilling lives, you'd be wrong.

Here's how things actually played out:

Dr. Sanders

Two years after the accident and still unemployed, Dr. Sanders was referred to me for vocational assistance. By then, a firm belief in her own disability had taken hold, and she could cite much research in support of her stance of total disability.

When I suggested she explore numerous sedentary jobs in the medical field that would benefit from her extensive expertise, she objected: "I don't feel I am employable at all ... there just isn't any work for someone who cannot stand for more than a few minutes."

She finally retreated with her ace in the hole, chronic pain, and spent many more hours researching a new disorder currently being hotly debated in medical circles: chronic pain syndrome. Her pain was real, but she used the new label to bolster her barriers against change.

One day, I showed her a striking black-and-white photo of an old man sporting a cowboy hat and short-sleeved shirt that exposed his muscular arms and gnarled, callused hands. The reason for his calluses was obvious: This man got around by using *only* his hands; he had no legs at all.

Dr. Sanders stared silently at the photo. Here stood a man whose body literally stopped at his hips, hopping along the sidewalk on his hands and hip sockets! Alongside him was his three-year-old grandson, who stood taller than he and who gently held his grandpa's shoulder as they "walked" along.

I explained to her that this man happened to have become a deputy sheriff and father well *after* he lost his legs.

Dr. Sanders seemed quite moved. As it turned out, however, nothing in her world changed. She remained stuck in a pattern commonly seen in chronically disabled people—an identification with her injury, a focus on disability and barriers, and *no clear purpose.*

Vivienne

Finally, Vivienne elected to go ahead with a mastectomy. During treatment after the surgery, however, she experienced an allergic drug reaction and became exceedingly ill for about eighteen hours. "I knew it was the morphine, but it took the hospital staff a while to figure it out. I finally just stopped taking the stuff."

When Vivienne's pain increased, she underwent a horrendous ordeal.

> *I experienced thirty-six hours of watching the clock. Not dozing. Not daydreaming. Just watching the second hand. For thirty-six hours.*
>
> *I did everything I knew how to do. I prayed, meditated. I can take myself out of here and place myself elsewhere when I'm bored or filled with anxiety—I have always*

been able to do that. But this time I couldn't do anything but just stay in all that pain for all that time.

Now you could look at that and you would say it was a terrible experience. However, after they found a way to control the pain again, I asked, "Hey God, or whatever you call yourself, where were you?"

And the answer was, "Well, you are still here. And I'm still here."

I felt like I was clearly in my body for the first time ever. So I can say that thirty-six hours was terrible. Yeah, it was awful. Would I take it back and not have it? Certainly not!

Paradoxically, Vivienne has come to treasure her ordeal as marking a profound shift in her awareness:

That is where the process really began. It was like moving from the spot of deciding what I was going through at the time was a bad scene to not having any judgment about it. I could simply go into the experience, whatever was there.

By the time I met her, Vivienne viewed life entirely differently:

Life has become more intense, more real. My creativity has vastly increased. There isn't enough time in the day practically. I've always been a pretty intense personality. The passion with which I do things is wild. I spent a lot of time in my life protecting this little person inside that was always damaged by things that happened on the outside. I finally decided to hell with that.

Roger

The antidepressants took the edge off Roger's black depression, but he took no direct action to reach out and engage socially, or to become more active physically and mentally.

One day, he twisted wrong, sending shooting pain to his hip. Although he was treated with steroid shots and he continued working, his pain finally overwhelmed him. As I entered his tool shop one afternoon, I saw that his hands trembled so much he could hardly hold his tools.

He looked at me with a desperate look I'd seen before. We sat down and talked for some time about how he could loosen his burden by making some lifestyle changes or pursuing more modifications to his job, but he'd parry every suggestion with reasons why it wouldn't work.

Roger felt he was a burden to his family. His body was deteriorating and the pain never let up. Life was skidding downhill…

We discussed how his attitude and perspective supported these beliefs and how he then reacted from them. Even though he was very conscientious and creative in his work, Roger couldn't translate his ability to create beautifully detailed and precise tools into ways of lifting himself beyond depression.

Although his physical therapist had given him many exercises he could do, Roger felt his doctor cancelled these out because he'd restricted Roger to walking only two hundred feet per day. Another no-win proposition.

Roger admitted there were options to engage socially, but for the many months we worked together, he never once took action to change his situation. Talking seemed to help a bit, but he remained clearly agitated.

During one session in my office, he suddenly pointed to the window and said, "Jim, turn around. Look at that." I looked up beyond the shadows of towering firs to see the setting sun enveloping the tip of a snow-clad mountaintop jutting majestically into the sky's rosy glow.

We gazed in awe as the sun finally melted beneath the earth's edge. Slowly the darkening sky settled around us, and we turned to each other again. No words could bridge the chasm that separated suffering from the promise of peace, but, visibly softened, we closed our meeting and quietly bade each other farewell.

When Roger didn't show up for work the following day, his boss called to let me know that a neighbor had discovered him sitting peacefully in front of his TV, dead.

No Judgment

The stories of Dr. Sanders and Roger, as well as my own story of lingering disability, show the emotional and psychic cost of attempting to struggle on under the burden of loss. Adapting to a new, more limited "normal" after a crisis event, people tend to assimilate disability or loss into their daily routine, often at a high cost to their quality of life.

The medical personnel who oversaw treatment for many of my clients spoke of two distinct patterns of response they observed in patients facing chronic disabilities: One group seemed to stay mired in their disability and experienced little change in perspective while the other re-engaged themselves in life and opened to new growth.

But these helping professionals were unable to predict who would fall into which group based on education, work history, upbringing, or financial status. Some vital but frustratingly intangible factor was at play—one noticed by most counselors, social workers, and other institutional caregivers.

To observe that some move onto a new "creation track" while others stay stuck is not to judge anyone, nor to prescribe a right way to respond to the panic of loss and chaos. It's possible, however, that if these two patterns of response were better identified and a creation track more generally recognized and supported, Dr. Sanders, Roger, and many others coping with crisis and chaos might seek the guideposts that would lead them to a more open-ended path.

Hanging Out in Limbo

In my own case, looking back, I understand better that my life as I knew it died that dark night the firefighter invaded my bedroom. The severe memory deficits and other limitations I faced after my catastrophic seizure in 1997 collapsed the world I knew as an avid mountain climber and skilled health professional. I now found even the simplest jobs difficult to sustain.

I accepted without question my doctor's pronouncement that adult brains don't heal and saw myself as permanently disabled.

Without any guideposts to tell me I was hanging on to shreds of my past at the edge of chaos, I grabbed onto a new identity and title: *Disabled*. There. Now I had a role that was understood and respected by others. My inability to contribute to my family's sustenance, to pursue a livelihood, or to be a contributing member of my community—all wrapped up in a tidy package that read: *Not my fault*.

The medical system itself had endowed me with that stamp, and my monthly disability check confirmed the sentence.

To be clear: I'm not saying the support I received wasn't warranted. Far from it. My family was able to survive a very difficult time because of the vital assistance from friends, family, the medical system, our insurance payments, and food assistance programs.

But now that I had fallen off the edge of my life and saw no medical miracle to lift me up or glue my life back together, I now felt I had no responsibility to contribute.

It's Really Gone

All my support flowed from the loss of myself as a productive, able-bodied person. No one met me at the bottom of the cliff, held me in my grief, and said:

This is who you are now. Trust that beyond your grief and pain and loss, new opportunities await. Feel the loss fully. Then, as you can, let go of comparing who you are now to what you were at the top of the cliff, where you could measure your worth through a profession, income, and accomplishments now beyond your reach. It's gone. Past. For good.

As you can, look at what you already have this very moment. You can see. You can walk and talk. You have desires. Follow them. Beyond the wilderness of loss, new creations and experiences await your taking action. **But you do have to act.** *Release your attachment to your past and let it go to the chaos of the unknown before you. No one can create a new life for you.*

So go ahead: If you could dream, what would you dream? If you could take a step, in what direction would you start? Whether or not you act or sit captured by your grief and loss, you're actively creating the life you're experiencing now.

Like me, many people remain identified by their losses after surviving a crisis. If they frame solutions in terms of the precrisis state, and if they cannot perform at that level again, they too see themselves as "less than," a victim, or disabled. Comparing themselves to what no longer exists keeps them experiencing the present in terms of their handicap. Now they have a new "normal." Chaos defeated!

It's Only the Middle, Not the End?

In the broadest terms, chaos and disorder can best be understood when book-ended by the larger processes of human growth. Researchers label chaos as a period "betwixt and between," "limbo," or the "liminal zone." These terms all define chaos in the context of a precrisis and postcrisis state.

We all know times of crisis and creative spurts, including the ever-popular "terrible twos," "teenage rebellion," or "midlife crisis," as well as less predictable periods of intense change. In between, most of us have also experienced trying periods of stuckness, lost-ness, or inertia in our lives—even so-called dark nights of the soul—that seemed endless. Oftentimes these will occur while we are negotiating a new life passage, and can entail much resistance.

It's only when such times of turmoil are well past that we un-derstand we were actually in the middle of something profoundly changing. At some point, we finally moved past our fear or resis-tance or lack of clarity, allowing for new growth.

Along the way, epiphany may open a dramatic new window of perception and understanding. Most of the time, however, the dance of chaos and order leading to higher levels of understand-ing or complexity plays out unobserved by us, cloaked within our everyday lives. The "you" looking through eyes reading these words today is the same "you" at fourteen years old, say, anx-iously attending your first school dance; the same "you" at seven years old, playing hopscotch; and the same "you" at two months old, staring at your mother changing your diaper.

But in most ways you now engage life from entirely different levels—emotionally, mentally, and physically. The flux of being in limbo, or chaos, keys the transformation bit by bit, nudging your life story in new directions—or sometimes prompting pain-filled, confusing leaps.

Then it resettles again into stasis.

Out of the Fire—and Back Again

And so we settle back into our own stories until something un-toward comes along and causes us to zig instead of zag. Looking back, I can discern how two experiences twenty-five years ago powerfully reshaped the rest of my life and set me on course to my present-day goals.

The beginning can be traced to an ending—divorce. Feeling depressed, with no viable career yet to anchor my life and no steady income or place to call home, I felt diminished and trapped. I thought about returning to school—at least that might provide some credibility I felt my life was lacking. But I had no job and no means to pay tuition, let alone pay my monthly rent and expenses.

What I did have was a keen interest in exploring systems-oriented psychology. At the time, three schools in the country offered the type of courses that strongly attracted me. One school was only a few miles away but might as well have been in Manchuria, as it was a private university charging exorbitant tuition.

Then one day I found myself wandering its grounds during quarter break. It was a small, urban satellite campus tucked into the city's hub—not much to look at, but with a comfortable feel to it.

Even before I reached the main office in search of further information, something had shifted inside me. A strange new feeling welled up ... excitement? ... relief? It made no sense but it brought a warm blessing like a newly lit candle into the darkened hollow of my depression.

Barriers vaporized. Suddenly I was "home," grounded in new purpose: *School.* Here. Now. Galvanized into action, I took out student loans, applied for grants, and installed myself in class at the start of a fresh new quarter. Nothing could diminish my focus. The invigorating feeling of following a clear purpose now pervaded my days.

By my second year, however, this passion and clarity had gradually melted away. A realization dawned that my capacity to envision new futures far outpaced the stolid progress of classrooms and textbooks. I wasn't finding answers there. In fact, my studies led me to the stark realization that the level of truth I sought cannot possibly be contained within a text or theory or belief.

This awareness both excited and distressed me. Feeling increasingly isolated, burdened by chronic pain from a back injury, and no longer engaged by my courses, I was burning out.

Which Way? Which Way?

One day, a friend (now my wife) suggested taking a day or two off to regain my clarity of purpose. After mulling it over a couple of days, even though final exams loomed, I decided to act. School, education, religious teachings—all had fallen short of the level of truth I was seeking. Besides, the fact was that people far worse off financially, educationally, and socially than I seemed happy and engaged with life. What was their key?

My old companions, Depression and Sadness, rode along with me as I set out in my dilapidated twelve-year-old station wagon with its broken driver's seat. Perhaps this was not the best treatment for a back injury, but my crisis and quest for meaning took precedence—how to access deeper truths than what words and beliefs and theories can possibly convey.

A day later, I reached the cloud-laden surf along Washington's ocean coast, opening enough distance between my present thoughts and past agenda to see more clearly. I began to grasp that my head and my intellect could never succeed in getting me to the truths I sought. The readings and teaching of scientists, philosophers, and mystics throughout the ages all point to higher truths accessible only by direct experience—thinking or reading or writing or believing will forever fall short.

But what else did I have? How else could I make choices but from my own thoughts, what I'd been taught, what others had shown me?

Even though only one week remained until final exams, I resolved to find an answer to my dilemma. So I headed south along Highway 101, hugging the edge of the Pacific coast, determined to drive all the way down to Mexico unless something besides my thoughts turned me around.

Within a day of poking along the edge of the ocean, my previously intense immersion in school washed away, exposing a sea of anguish as wave after wave of numbing angst washed over me. At each stop and each Y in the road, I asked, *Where am I going? How can I get there? What's to guide me?*

I had entered a strange, directionless world.

After several days of aimless wandering, I crawled up on a huge boulder where the Columbia River dissolves into the limitless ocean. Brown and white spume rocketed off the crests of the waves as they tossed themselves heedlessly against the rocks. The rhythm of the waves and the seagulls floating so silently above somehow calmed me. I felt I could stay there forever.

Reflexively, as I'd been trained to do in all those philosophy courses and wisdom texts, I applied myself to observing my own thought processes. What exactly was it that propelled me to take *any* action or entertain a particular thought?

But fighting hard for my full attention was the urgent call to get back to reality, walk straight back to my car, point it north, and drive back home as fast as I could to complete school. Which brought on the usual objections: *To accumulate the goods and services of our civilization? To find a good job and climb the ladder of "success"? To work hard and then die?*

I strove to attain possessions, success, and recognition, because I was taught to value them.

But to what end, really?

In my car once again with its dilapidated seat and with my back hurting more and more, I began to despair of ever finding a way forward. A profound realization seeped through me like contaminated water poisoning my mind: *Everything you've struggled for in life, everything you've done to attain some higher level of safety and self-worth, means exactly* nothing.

Wiping the Slate Clean

It was at the cliff edge near Heceta Head on the coast of Oregon where something happened that to this day I cannot fully grasp.

I had climbed atop a secluded rocky cliff overlooking the crashing ocean waves. Emptiness and meaninglessness lay stretched endlessly before me. Standing on the cliff's edge, I looked at the pounding surf crashing into the rocks 250 feet below me. I looked at the path leading back to my car.

Two choices loomed in front of me. I could make the choice to gently push off the cliff's edge, freefall a few long seconds until that moment I met the surface of the jagged, surf-drenched rocks below. Beyond that point of impact, what would my experience be? Shreds of beliefs torn from the pages of my past—church teaching, scientific theories, wonderings and wanderings of my mind, all useless. What *really* lay beyond that moment of impact?

Or, I could choose to turn toward the path leading to my car, slide uncomfortably into that broken seat, slip the key in the ignition, and drive away. But where to? For what purpose? In tears, a profound angst overwhelmed me.

Then, without warning, I heard a voice.

It said, simply, "It's important for you to experience this, for others."

I whirled around. There was nothing except the cliff edge framing sky and sea and seagulls gliding quietly in the updrafts behind me. Nothing else.

A message from God? A psychotic break? All I knew was that this voice was as clear and real as if a person were standing right behind me.

Confused and disoriented, I peered over the cliff edge, then toward the trail back to my car, wondering where it might take me. I wasn't ready for that final moment in a physical body, so I slowly made my way back to the highway.

I Was Already "There"

Days later and a hundred miles further south, I lay down in the warming sun near the redwoods in California and dozed off, my head pillowed by the roots of an ancient giant. I think that's where a tick must have found me, but alas, Enlightenment did not.

Yet I awakened to a newfound inner calmness, reflected in the soft, salt-cleansed breeze brushing my face. The question "What to do?" immediately seized center stage. Only now as I performed my ritual of looking south to Mexico and north to school, I sensed that this part of my journey was complete.

The calmness and the freshening breeze had carried something else to me: Although it was barely discernible, I sensed a new pathway opening up. Somehow I knew my formal schooling was over—this trip my thesis. Over the years I've come to see that deep within the desperation of those dark days, a new integration of thought and emotion had already begun to coalesce, turning me toward an unscripted future.

Two Who Walked Away

For a deeper perspective, let's turn to more exalted examples of chaos birthing the new. Consider that the Christian story of Jesus wandering forty days and nights in the wilderness wasn't a story at all when he set out to seek a higher truth. The world around him was unable to contain the questions or provide a path to the answers he sought. So he left, just walked away from the social and religious structures of his day, guided only by his restless desire to seek a deeper reality.

Jesus consciously plunged into the unknown. No sure direction, outcome, or answers existed at the start of his journey. Only in hindsight does the story wrap itself around a beginning, a period of upheaval, and a new stabilization and awareness at a higher level.

Similarly, the Buddhist story of the young prince Siddhartha recounts a journey of life-changing discovery from a very different vantage. Protected from any want and indulged in all his desires, Siddhartha nevertheless grew restless. Finally he escaped his safe, cloistered existence in his father's palace, an episode now known as "The Great Departure."

Siddhartha made bold to go among the people and learn the worst about human suffering, death, and disease. He became an ascetic, begging for alms and searching for the true meaning of life. Like Jesus, in his search for a higher truth, he rejected offers of earthly power and leadership. Instead he endured years of self-mortification and deprivation before finally attaining what he called enlightenment.

Again, only in retrospect does the story weave itself in three parts: leaving the known, entering a period of confusion and searching, and discovering a more expanded expression of life than was previously possible.

And if we ponder the matter seriously, we can see how these master teachers' simple, transformational message of present-moment awareness has been overtaken by religious doctrines, prescribed rituals, and traditions—reassuring anchors of certainty against the chaos of an ungraspable whole.

Still, like Jesus and Siddhartha, each one of us has the power to assume a perspective untethered from our background and circumstances and make fresh choices from it. We can choose again and again, moment by moment, to step into the unknown.

Chapter 3
When Chaos Brings Transformation

There is a palace that opens only to tears.

— Rumi —

For Roger the final chapter of his life story was written and sealed. Crisis degraded his ability to see the possibility of fulfillment and engagement in his life. Dr. Sanders was going down the same futureless path. But for Vivienne and many others, the collapse of their lives proved only a chapter in a much larger story containing some unexpected twists and turns, and an even more surprising transformation in quality.

From this point forward, we'll be looking more closely at the second group—let's call them conscious *choice makers.* Here are the stories of two more who were pushed off the edge.

Taking the Plunge—Jeff's Story

An intensely competitive athlete, Jeff had just started his junior year in football and worked his way up to first-string defense. Anxious to impress his coaches in a key game, he tried to butt his helmet into an opponent's stomach to "really knock him for a loop." But instead he hit the other player's quadriceps just as he pumped his legs. Jeff's head snapped back.

He found himself looking up at the sky with his neck burning, and he blurted, "I got a concussion—don't know what's going on."

He remembers:

I could see my arms lying straight out beside me. I could see them there and remembered thinking, "What's going on here?" So I asked my coach, "Where are my legs?" He said, "Well, they're lying on the ground."

That was the first time I knew something was really wrong. The coaches wouldn't touch me. They didn't take my helmet off but immediately ran across the street and called an ambulance.

In the hospital, an emergency medical team cut off Jeff's football gear. He told me:

It happened so fast. The next thing I knew, they were drilling holes in the side of my head above my ears. They didn't put you to sleep to drill the holes, they just numbed it … and I could feel the blood dripping down the side of my face. You know, I still had absolutely no idea of what was going on—just that it was serious.

Very serious. In the blink of an eye, a misbegotten football move had left Jeff, age seventeen, a quadriplegic.

"I'll See You in the Morning"

Jeff's family never left his side after the accident. He distinctly remembers being wheeled into surgery because the doctor told him, "Now Jeff, I've got to be perfectly honest with you. You have a one-in-one-thousand chance of pulling through this surgery."

Without hesitation, Jeff told him: "Let's go for it. I'll see you in the morning." With that simple intention, he dove straight into the heart of chaos.

After surviving the surgery, Jeff began a new life at Children's Hospital in Seattle. He told me:

This was probably the toughest time in my entire life because I had to learn everything all over again. Even after multiple surgeries, I could move absolutely nothing except my mouth and my eyes.

I wanted to go back to school and graduate with my class… When I was stable enough to return to school I found a lot of obstacles in the way of learning. The first one was: How do I turn a page? The second one was: Okay, how do I take notes in class?

Jeff pointed out a number of things that helped keep him going, including a teenage girl his age, Karen, who was also left quadriplegic after breaking her neck in a diving accident. She was slightly ahead of him in her recovery. As Karen successfully navigated each new step, Jeff followed. "We got so that we fed off each other, and I think that helped each of us a lot," he recalls.

At the time Jeff was discharged after six or seven months, his doctor told him his life expectancy was about ten or fifteen years. It's now been over thirty years since the accident. At the time I met him, Jeff was working as the director of the Resource Center for the Handicapped, on loan from the Boeing Company, which sponsors a community service program that lends executives to community organizations. A quiet but confident man, clearly used to being in charge, Jeff looks like any other executive, except that he works from his wheelchair.

Jeff was one who didn't second-guess his fate. Unlike so many who experience the collapse of what they cherished, he seems never to have looked back. Maybe it was his reckless youth or the fact that he hadn't yet established much of an identity to lose. Who can say? Somehow he managed to stare down his futureless future and say: "Bring it on!" In what seemed a situation of total helplessness, Jeff took an active stance toward the future—an attitude that has made all the difference.

Crash Landing into Chaos—Joan's Story

One January morning in 1991, a private plane carrying Joan and piloted by her husband Ted took off from a small runway in North Carolina. Almost immediately it developed engine problems. Ted had often said he could land anywhere provided he had altitude—and this was the problem—engine failure and lack of enough altitude. The plane flipped up into a stand of nearby trees, where it lodged upside down. Ted died on impact; Joan sustained grave injuries, including severe brain trauma.

Each day after the accident, Joan relived the trauma of learning from her sister Doris that Ted had died in the plane crash. Each day, she forgot. She would repeatedly ask, "What happened to Ted? Where did he go? Is he dead?"

Finally, one day about a month after the accident, Doris finally gathered the courage to show Joan photos of the crash site. The wings and fuselage were torn but the plane was recognizable as Ted's.

The reality of Ted's death slowly took hold. Joan grieved the loss of her husband and devastation of her life. Her physical challenges were enormous:

> I couldn't remember much and had difficulty speaking and walking. I was so dizzy I'd fall if I turned my head to either side, so I learned to turn my whole body so as not to become so disoriented I'd fall down.

She couldn't walk or drive without assistance or practice her violin because the notes kept moving around on the page.

Joan recalls:

> Denial slowed my progress for some time. I didn't think anything was wrong. I thought I just didn't want to go home without Ted. Even though I felt I was fine, I couldn't

remember simple words. I'd talk about things like, "the thing with the four wheels."

She had convinced herself that she was fooling everyone about her brain damage:

I felt I was making it all up as a way to stay in the hospital. I simply didn't want to go home by myself and face being home without my husband. I was randomly incontinent in my wheelchair and thought that was "normal."

Finally one doctor told me angrily that if I worked as a nurse in the hospital for him, I would be fired since I couldn't remember even simple things. That finally got my attention. When I did go home, I didn't recognize any of my own things. I didn't recognize my own belongings—it was like somebody else was living in my home. I felt terribly alone.

Grounded

Whereas Jeff was ready to plunge into an unknown future, Joan definitely was not. Her losses—including a solid sense of self— left her feeling not only alone but suicidal. She reasoned that if she wasn't around, her kids could have it all, and she wouldn't be an imposition on her friends and family. But when she realized the course she had set, her mind turned a corner. She decided to take some positive action on her own behalf:

When I figured a way to end it all, the old nurse part of me kicked in and said, "Joan, now is the time to ask for help." I had been getting psychological help all along for the grief and head deficits, but at that time I was alone at the lake. So I called the psychologist and told him about my plans. He listened and I talked. I said all I wanted to do when they let me drive to the lake is sit on the dock and cry all day. He gave permission and said "Do it!" so as not to solve a temporary problem with a permanent solution.

Eventually Joan opened to the help of friends and family:

Sometimes I cried for days. I talked to lots of girlfriends. My sister and mom were very supportive and encouraged me to get out more. I decided to build a house on the land where we had a small vacation cabin on the lake. It contained so many memories. Even the neighbors at the lake helped advise me so I called it a house built by "committee."

Joan remained disabled for some time before truly taking hold of her new life. As in my own case, Joan's brain eventually recovered to a degree unexpected by her doctors. Her perspective on her ordeal and how she thought about rebuilding her life began to shift. She became more and more self-reliant:

I was determined not to rely on others and be a burden—stubborn, yes—it all took years. I could feel Ted's presence nearby for a long time, but now it's quite distant, almost seventeen years now.

Changing Our Lens to Post-Traumatic Growth

Researchers over the last several decades have examined the power of crisis to impact lives positively. People who remain fixed on reclaiming their lives as they were precrisis often stay stuck in limitation, but clear patterns can be perceived among those who actually do grow through crisis.

These individuals share so many distinct characteristics that the growth pattern they demonstrate has been termed post-traumatic growth (PTG). We are much more familiar with PTSD (post-traumatic stress disorder), resulting from severe or prolonged trauma—an often severe problem that dogs a person for an entire lifetime.

Interestingly, I've seen people that suffer from PTSD also eventually exhibit the pattern associated with PTG. They may still react to certain events that trigger the old *symptoms*. But their symptoms do not prevent stunning growth and expansion into new arenas of self-expression and success.

In view of the many thousands of war veterans returning from Iraq and Afghanistan with symptoms or diagnoses of PTSD, it's especially urgent that this wonderful growth pattern of post-traumatic growth be systematically researched and supported.

What Makes People Grow?

In 1983, Ronnie Janoff-Bulman and Irene Frieze examined basic assumptions people typically make regarding the meaningfulness of life and their own self-worth. They then asked: What happens when trauma or crisis severely challenges these assumptions?

These researchers were able to confirm that some people became stronger and more emotionally stable after such trauma. Some even characterized the crisis or traumatic event as a spiritual awakening. Janoff-Bulman and Frieze also observed that this type of growth through crisis resulted from subjects' *willingness to change core beliefs that had previously governed their lives.*[1]

During the 1990s, other researchers such as R. G. Tedeschi and L. G. Calhoun, both professors of psychology at the University of North Carolina, identified striking similarities among those who grow through crisis, including changes in perceived personal strength, emotional stability, self-reliance, and assertiveness, as well as greater appreciation of life.

They also observed common by-products in the wake of trauma: a new philosophy of life, increased spirituality and care for others, family cohesiveness, and stronger relationships.

An Inside-Out Process

Tedeschi and Calhoun observed that growth through trauma results from the internal struggle to confront a reality no longer tenable or readily assimilated, and is *not* associated with the problem itself. Their findings indicate that profound shifts in a person's outlook and sense of well-being spring more from internal changes rather than from the type of trauma experienced. Many subjects found that coping with their crisis led to higher levels of well-being.[2]

Attempts to tie PTG to predisposing factors such as hardiness, extroversion, past experience, and education levels show contradictory results. It's unclear in the research which predisposing factors, if any, are required for growth. But it is clear that at some point individuals who move into PTG take responsibility to try on new ways of perceiving themselves and their situations. They then act on their openness to new possibilities.

Traditional therapies typically do not take into account the spiritual dimension that subjects of PTG research so often express—people commonly describe an expansion beyond being tethered to any particular religious belief system. This expansion becomes embodied in their heightened appreciation for life and affirming attitudes towards others.

Partnering with Paradox

Historically, psychology and medicine have focused almost entirely on disease identification and elimination, operating on the assumption that once all the problems are eliminated, well-being will ensue. However, PTG research clearly discloses growth in the wake of trauma and loss—a counterintuitive outcome that confounds explanation. This is especially so since those who undergo the most disruption and loss in their lives often experience the most inner growth.

Once an individual becomes able to acknowledge both the negative and positive aspects of life after suffering a trauma, she or he shows an increased ability to respond in health-giving ways.

Jack Bauer, a psychologist at Northern Arizona University, followed individuals for several years after the death of a spouse. Those who flourished most after losing their partner expressed more positive than negative memories. However, their ability to express the negative was important as well. If a surviving spouse tended to focus only on the negative *or* exclusively on the positive—he or she remained compromised.[3]

Is PTG Real or Imagined?

The counterintuitive and paradoxical nature of PTG causes many of us to wonder how gifts of growth actually emerge from crisis. Is the perception of growth only the product of self-preserving rationalization? Or just a smiley face pasted over one's past?

I thought this myself when I first started interviewing people in the 1980s. But then I started listening more closely. These people were telling me consistently that, in retrospect, only *after* experiencing their terminal illness, divorce, lost career, lost limbs, or a lost child, were they able somehow to open to new possibilities and expanded states of being.

PTG researchers observe the same pattern. Not only do people retrospectively see growth and higher levels of well-being, but they also are emphatic about the benefits that come in the wake of their trauma. They simultaneously acknowledge and accept any residual problems and limitations that now confront them. Researchers have so often identified this pattern that they conclude it is unlikely to be a mere product of rationalization.

A Cautionary Note

The introduction of the potential growth inherent in crisis may present an additional burden on the person in the depths of despair and grief. When an individual is already feeling crushed, trapped, or defeated, the addition of yet another "goal" to achieve can be a setup for more feelings of failure. Facilitating growth requires a different relationship between the person in crisis and surrounding helpers, one that allows for the full acceptance of present reality.

The turning point for many occurs when they truly accept that the problem is *unfixable*. (In Chapter 9, we will investigate how the caregiver can effectively help the person shift from a disability perspective to ability-based focus on becoming the creative force in his or her own life, regardless of circumstance.)

Each person's journey is unique and plainly does not conform to a standard procedure or timeline. It's neither helpful nor authentic to compare one person's journey with another's. For every choice maker, transformational dynamics work their magic *over time*. Most often, growth can only be discerned in retrospect, as new perspectives consolidate into dramatically changed ways of being with oneself and one's surroundings.

Dramatic Change in Self-Concept—Vivienne

As someone who underwent profound changes in self-concept via her journey through crisis and chaos, Vivienne stands out as a role model for PTG. Like many who embark on a self-powered creation track, she experienced greatly enhanced self-reliance, assertiveness, and appreciation for life.

Under threat of the surgeon's knife, this "Teacher of the Year" now confronted the truth about herself: She'd been a lifelong depressive, putting on a happy face for her many "friends."

> *I always felt I was really open, but I wasn't. I had a lot of friends—always a lot of friends. My close relationships were more difficult. I felt I had to be something special in order to keep people around in my life. So I did a lot of acting… other people determined who I was.*
>
> *Most of my life was spent depressed on some level or another… How people saw me on the outside was vastly*

*different from what I felt on the inside...I knew inside
that whatever I did was wrong.*

Judgments about myself swamped me.

Learning To Assert Herself

Getting honest with herself and those around her, Vivienne became much more assertive and began to trust her own judgments. Her family naturally expected her to feel frightened about the impending mastectomy, and they kept reassuring her there couldn't be anything malignant going on. This made her angry—*finally:*

> *I said to my mother, "What do you mean it can't be malignant? It can be! It can be whatever it is!" I think probably for the first time in my life I decided I wasn't going to let anybody tell me how I felt about things. I was going to feel it myself. And I was not afraid. This was a very significant change in my life.*

Coming Clean

Once she accepted what was happening, Vivienne confronted her core beliefs about her life and how, as an adult, her actions and beliefs were choreographed by a negative image of herself. When asked what kind of judgments she held about herself, she responded:

> *My judgments about myself? I was always a mess, always felt dumb. Whenever I achieved anything I felt I was dishonest. Always inadequate. I could stay up until three in the morning and start again at five in the morning. No matter how much I did, it was not enough.*
>
> *Most of my life was spent depressed on some level or another. I am a very good actor, and I could even act for myself sometimes, but most of the time I experienced depression of some kind...My relationships with people*

were from acting out roles. But I knew that whatever I did was wrong.

I had the mastectomy. I wasn't afraid. It was more like I was numb. People said I was so courageous, but I was just numb to all the events. I was still searching at that time. It didn't seem to matter very much what happened. My mother was unhappy she wasn't at the center of my healing and that I didn't go stay at her house. I was outraged. I had to deal with her healing rather than mine. She's a lovely lady, but I had to deal with the fact I was saying things that would hurt her.

Why Cancer, Vivienne?

Vivienne told me that before her cancer, she had experienced a "terrifically hideous divorce" after which she literally had wanted to die. She recalls:

Two years later I started dating, feeling happy again, but discovered a lump in my breast. I didn't think anything of it, but I knew it had to be taken care of. I was absolutely dumbfounded about the diagnosis of malignancy.

I asked Vivienne if she thought her cancer might have been there for a purpose. Her answer reflected her growth and learning from the ordeal:

I wouldn't will it or wish it out of my life for anything. Not for anything. My real relationship with people is that the moment we are here together will never exist again. We could duplicate everything about the experience together, but we could not possibly recapture the experience itself. For me, cancer was a process for setting up a way for me to understand that.

She reflected how the inner change took hold.

There was no single transformational event. The change took place over a long period of time... in the process I began to insert myself more into my own life. What was important was knowing. Being right now.

I mean, it's really unimportant to me if I discover today that I have a lump and that I'll be dead in two months. It's just not important. (Laughter) I know it sounds awful, but it just isn't important. It's not an issue. I would go in and do whatever has to be done about the tumor, but the living and the dying are not important.

What is important is what happens this day. I know that sounds like Pollyanna. I sound stupid to myself even, but that's where it's at. I'm sorry. This is it! Right now, I feel wonderful. And if I didn't, I would figure out a way to support my body as best I could.

The cancer is not an issue. I do not think I will get cancer again, but if I do, it will be because the cancer needs to be there for some reason. I don't know where it comes from— whether I generate it or the universe generates it or whether it's simply there. I don't understand, but it doesn't matter. What matters is the quality of how I do whatever it is I do.

A Life on Wheels—Jeff Looks Back

Like Vivienne, Jeff made a dramatic shift in how he saw himself and his immediate world. He could no longer view the journey from the eyes of a strapping young athlete, running, tackling, excelling in movement. Instead he was required to see possibility and purpose while forever limited to rolling in a wheelchair.

My attitude has always been pretty positive, which has helped me after the accident and being confined to a wheelchair. I think a lot of that has to do with being brought up playing sports. They give you that competitive attitude, and you always want to strive to be the best that you can be.

I remember when I was playing football, I could hear people on the sidelines yelling and encouraging me to do better. Like I was running a race or something. The yelling and cheering—that meant so much to me. I didn't realize it at the time, but I can reflect back now and see how important it was. I did much better when people were cheering for me than when the stands were quiet, so I became a yeller and cheerer for others.

When I asked him if, looking back, he could see the impact of his injury on the quality and value of his life, Jeff revealed another signal characteristic of PTG: gratitude.

I thank God daily, who has allowed me this privilege to be a part of this life—to be able to contribute to other people's lives and help them, I think, become better people. I've got a lot of friends. They look up to me and they think I'm a good role model for others. To me, that's a compliment. People really want kids to know me and to learn from me. You know, that's exciting, and if I can touch somebody's life and make it better, it just really touches my heart to know I can do that. It gives me fulfillment. What keeps me going is knowing I can help other people. I'm actually part of their lives.

People will say things like, "Will you walk with me to the coffee machine?" or "Let's walk outside and talk." Then they catch themselves. "Oops, I'm sorry. I didn't mean to offend you." I say, "Look, you just paid me the highest compliment that you can ever pay me." Other people come up to me and make comments like, "Jeff, I don't even see you as being in a chair." That's a high compliment to me because that's how I perceive myself and that's how I want other people to perceive me ... I want them to look at me as being Jeff. I have as much capacity for joy and fulfillment as anyone else.

Joan Takes Flight Again

From a space of feeling worthless and at times suicidal during her recovery, Joan gradually evolved toward a whole new relationship with her life. I asked her how she regarded the tragedy of the plane crash from her current vantage, some seventeen years later. She told me:

I'm forever changed but have more gratitude each day than I ever had previously. I have gratitude for many aspects of life and thank God for each day. I was always somewhat of an agnostic before but am certain a higher power I choose to call God was very instrumental in my life and recovery. Even the doctors cannot tell me why I recovered as I have, as the brain was so very injured.

But I also have a great sadness for all the days Ted has missed. It is of some comfort that whenever I told him what a great nurse I was and would always care for him if needed, he would shake that finger at me and say, "Oh, no, I'd rather go in my airplane."

And I know he didn't suffer. Many times, however, I used to think he had the easy part compared to my struggles. But now I'm thankful for all I have.

Joan's expression of gratitude for the inner growth she has experienced since her losses didn't surprise me. I could tell by the way she spoke and held herself that, in retrospect, she would view the destruction of her former life as an opening to a more vibrant relationship with the world.

And so it was.

Chapter 4
The Creation Cycle

People are like stained glass windows.
They sparkle when the sun is out, but when
the darkness sets in, their true beauty is revealed
only if there is a light from within.

— *Elizabeth Kübler-Ross* —

We've been following a number of people whose journeys through crisis tore them loose from their moorings of meaning, security, and predictability and who either were defeated by their circumstances or experienced a shift in perspective that placed them on an altogether new developmental path.

The contrasts are stark: One group remained identified with what had been lost, and the other let go of what was threatened or lost and opened to the unknown, allowing themselves to be led to entirely new ways of being and acting.

The crisis-to-creation dynamics of post-traumatic growth that their stories disclose are powered by what I've termed the *Creation Cycle*, which this chapter sets out in some detail.

Arriving at a Choice Point

When individuals find themselves in chaos and confusion after a life-shattering crisis, some sort of choice point seems to inhere in that space of profound ungroundedness. A shift in perspective may occur—resulting in new choices. Or not, depending upon the individual's readiness to move on.

At this point, people in chaos will either *choose* to stay with the status quo, miserable as it may be, or launch into uncharted waters. *Their lives transform directly as a result of actions spurred by crisis.*

The Creation Cycle unfolds in three interblending phases:

- *Crisis and loss* threaten our identity, worth, or survival, followed by:

- *Chaos* of the unknown, from which may emerge a shift in awareness, resulting in:

- New actions, thus *new creations.*

Together these powerful dynamics create a deeper level of fulfillment than what existed in precrisis times.

Creation Dynamics at the Edges of Life

Perhaps the easiest way to see the Creation Cycle is at the edges of human experience, where we naturally move to new ways of understanding and interacting: If we enter life as healthy babies, we enter the world precrisis, without predisposition or belief. After birth, though, our lives from young to old bear a constant crisis of change.

Jean Piaget, a pioneer in developmental psychology, observed how children assimilate new experiences into their current beliefs. A child whose beliefs are challenged faces a dilemma: to either try to fit the new experience into an existing belief or drop the belief and stretch beyond the threshold of understanding to accommodate the new experience. [4]

We call this growth and maturation. In most of us, the urge to define ourselves as we mature confines and reduces this natural process of creation, leaving us to go through it all over again at the next sudden change or crisis.

At the other end of life's journey, there are choices to be made when leaving the world: to die content and at peace, or fighting what's happening to the last breath.

Gaining Strength at Death's Door

Renowned author and speaker Joan Borysenko, PhD, cofounder of the Mind/Body Clinic at Harvard University, observed a pattern of creating from crisis in her work with terminally ill patients. After learning their diagnosis, people often described feeling as if they were falling into the abyss.

Borysenko observes, "The shell of ego cracks, and its habitual way of constructing the world falters. Deprived of familiar frameworks, we are invited to enter the ritual process of transformation."[5]

Arrived at this point, some may surrender and let go of their hold on a particular "reality." Borysenko states, "We have died to who we were, but are not yet reborn to who we might become. We are at the doorway, the threshold of new potential."[6]

By inviting in the unknown, we allow inspired ways of seeing and being to blossom and grace our lives with awe. Strengths discovered in this chaos of transformation are powerful gifts we can bring back for the good of our family, community, and the world.

Coming Full Circle and Finding ... *More*

The essential elements in crisis-to-creation stories easily stand out. Each journey offers guideposts that reflect the three stages of the creation process, with ensuing changes in beliefs, desires, and actions. Artists readily recognize this cycle. Indeed, it manifests in our everyday activities that lead to change and growth. The visual below summarizes these dynamics.

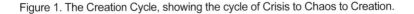

Figure 1. The Creation Cycle, showing the cycle of Crisis to Chaos to Creation.

The Creation Cycle

The cycle represents the dynamic flow of new creations, their dissolution into the fertile field of chaos from which new creations emerge, themselves eventually dissolving into new forms. The diagram represents:

Crisis: Fighting to retain or regain what is threatened or lost.

Chaos: Swirling within the upheaval and loss of meaning, direction, purpose.

Creation: Taking direct action toward a clear desire, opening to new ideas, actions, and levels of well-being.

CRISIS

A precipitating event or trigger brings loss and destruction of what we value. We may invest heavily in reclaiming or replacing what we once had. The extent of crisis is linked to the level of attachment and value we give to the loss. Our response to crisis manifests in predictable ways:

- Focus all available resources on restoring balance or fixing the problem.
- Feel trapped and limited by failure to regain the precrisis state.
- Grieve loss through expressions of denial, anger, depression, and despair.
- Feel victimized by lack of help to reclaim or regain what was lost.
- Experience helplessness and hopelessness.

Another way to view this stage is one of "collapsing realities," when a person's livelihood, worldly goods, or very life is threatened or destroyed. All resources are marshaled to stamp out the problem, or at least jam a finger into the dike to limit damages.

What follows collapsed realities is almost always…

CHAOS

Uncertainty ensues if crisis-centered efforts are ineffective to resolve problems. Chaos manifests when the individual experiences:

- Loss of focus or control.
- Disorientation and confusion about how to prioritize and organize.
- Loss of self—identity, value, purpose, meaning.

Letting go to chaos is one of the most challenging steps we human beings ever face because we can no longer engage our thoughts in any consistent or meaningful way. This loss of meaning and direction leads to feelings of angst, crisis of faith, a spiritual "dark night of the soul." What we called "normal" is lost, and we find ourselves wandering in the wilderness.

Note that in the crisis-to-creation stories recounted thus far, often it is only when no other options exist does the person let go to the confusion of chaos. Dramatic personal growth often ensues.

Thus chaos ultimately gives rise to…

CREATION

New impulses or desires bring expanded perspectives and relationships. Such desires refocus a person's attention on abilities already present, with the result that one sees oneself as able to create anew. Creation manifests as these individual experiences:

• Desires to explore or create without any need for healing.

• Actions focused on residual abilities already present.

• Focus on new relationships and new meanings surrounding events.

• Increased sense of well-being unconstrained by circumstances.

On the path from crisis to new creations, the individual may catch sight of new vistas, if only momentarily. The lens of old beliefs is suspended and eventually discarded as new creations take root. However, the Creation Cycle brings not just a rearrangement of the old, but a fundamental restructuring of present reality unconstrained by the tatters of the past.

In retrospect, the process of destruction and re-creation can be seen to yield higher levels of self-responsibility, creativity, and life satisfaction. Other outcomes commonly observed are a spontaneous, altruistic desire to be more positively engaged in the lives of others, greater willingness to resolve conflicts, and increased ability to reach beyond ambiguity and embrace paradox.

The three phases of the Creation Cycle thus meld into a *gestalt,* all woven together and interacting with one another. There is no linear step-by-step program to the cycle. Once our present circumstances are seen as part of a larger cycle, we become the master weaver, able to introduce a different *C* by choice into an expanding tapestry of new creations.

Headlong into Crisis—Evy McDonald's Story

One of the most powerful and conscious weavers I've had the privilege of befriending is a survivor of amyotrophic lateral sclerosis (ALS) named Evy, whom I first met in 1988. Since then she has become a model of possibility for me—especially during times when I saw none in my own life. On those occasions when I find myself trapped in a problem and unable to see a way out, her powerful story inevitably pops into my mind, and my problem loosens its tight grip.

Her story illuminates the three phases of the Creation Cycle seen in post-traumatic growth.

Evy confronted the crisis of her terminal diagnosis with ALS, or Lou Gehrig's disease, in 1981. At the time I had no knowledge of the disease or its course, or even how to pronounce it. (Today, most people know ALS because of the man who sits in Einstein's chair at Cambridge: Stephen Hawking. Dr. Hawking continues to awe the world with his courage and grace, living a productive life in spite of being quadriplegic and unable to speak.)

As a young health professional, Evy steadily rose through the ranks of healthcare to become director of intensive care and coronary care at the University of Washington Hospital. She had set her sights on becoming the youngest female hospital administrator in the country. Looking back, she admitted this goal may have been generated in part by her desire to overcome a physical disability stemming from childhood polio. She strove for outer success in the professional world to compensate for her handicap and self-described imperfections.

However, the diagnosis of ALS not only derailed her career but also stamped her as terminally ill with an incurable, untreatable disease. Before her diagnosis, she limped on a leg deformed by her childhood polio. Now, she faced a much greater enemy—a deteriorating body slowly imprisoning her in a wheelchair on a one-way journey to certain death.

Letting Go to Chaos

Evy watched her body gradually lose function as the disease ravaged her nervous system. Diabolically, her mental functions remained totally intact even as her nerves slowly severed connections between her body and brain. Her anger at the unfairness finally got the best of her. She later wrote:

> *I thought, what do I do from here? What are the steps I take? The first thing I did was have a fit. At this point I still had a cane and could use one arm and used a wheelchair. I went to my room, closed the door, and very quietly, tore the place apart. I didn't want anyone to know what I was doing. I didn't want to disturb anybody. I broke lamps with my cane, broke bottles on my dresser. I tore clothes. I destroyed my past. When in high school and college, I won all sorts of awards—I destroyed as much as possible. I totally, totally, completely exhausted myself... I let it all go.*

Evy has expressed frustration when others try to analyze what triggered her cure from ALS, as she recently emphasized to me.

> *I never wanted to cure myself—that was not a goal, nor was it a thought. When I was dying every moment of the day, trying to have the best death ever—as only an overachiever can want to do—I had no thought of cure.*

Similar frustrations were voiced to me years earlier in our discussions, and they can be seen throughout her writings. She was consistent in stating that her goal was not to find a cure, but to learn to love before she died:

> *The first question I asked myself was, "Who did I want to be when I died?" It was not someone famous, but someone who knew and accepted love—neither of which I could do.*
>
> *That was when I truly began a spiritual journey—to learn how to love a body I had always hated and to learn how to accept love from others that I had successfully blocked out.*
>
> *… I was no longer angry or fearful about death—that was in the future. We are all terminal. If I was living each second, each breath, each moment, I could be fully present then, and I would not need to be concerned about past or future. I wanted my life to be about giving… I was going beyond ego that wanted attention, taking, needy. This was very subtle—I wanted to go beyond that person who was never satisfied.*
>
> *One day I looked up the definition of "perfect" in* Webster's Dictionary: *(1) Having all the properties naturally belonging to it. Complete.*
>
> *It's not some standard step one through ten until you get it right. It's everything you are at that point… no matter what your body is doing right now, no matter its state. I began to love for the first time. I began to see the strength and power that we all have.*
>
> *There came a moment when it was as if a switch had been turned on—it was after a lot of hard work—when I looked at my body with its different sizes (one leg was so much smaller from polio) and saw beauty.*

"Jell-O in a Wheelchair"

Paradoxically, even as Evy watched her body deteriorate slowly, day by day, a newfound aliveness sprang from within.

> *At this point new thoughts came flooding in. It was as if the floodgates opened. I now had room not to die every moment. I now could live. It didn't make any difference how much time I had left. If I was in a wheelchair totally dependent on others for daily living, it didn't make a difference to me. It was like something being lifted off my chest. I could live. I could love. I could be joyful. I could be happy looking just like I was—Jell-O in a wheelchair.*
>
> *So at each moment I chose to live, to love, and be. From that honest sense of "I love me," I didn't need to be different. I chose to be happy. I became filled with vitality. That was something I could give to anyone in my presence—my vitality.*
>
> *I found love and happiness does not have to equate to form. I found my physical form could be just whatever it was. I could be in a wheelchair... I could be unable to lift my arms, and I could still be in the spirit of love and joy... That would always be solid. Those things are the solid things in life, and the forms we think are solid, like bodies, are what change all the time.*
>
> *I also found I could choose to be happy without suppressing other feelings.*

Thriving Even While NOT Surviving

Without exception, everyone I interviewed over the last twenty years discovered a gift or new richness in the crises they transited through, even if the crisis-triggering problems failed to be defeated. As these people let go of their attachment to the past, they naturally and radically changed the direction of their lives in the process. They went from focusing all their attention on mere survival or elimination of the problem to embracing a richer, more fulfilling life experience, despite the continuing outer limitations.

When their stories are closely examined, the ability of these people to create from loss and chaos seem to challenge common sense. Isn't it well-assumed that only when people's basic survival needs are met that they will start expressing elements of higher-level living, such as compassion, service, spirituality, creativity, and so forth?

Yet, here is what was found even in terminally ill people who embraced the entire Creation Cycle: Once they realized they had nowhere to go, and no control over their fate, they released their focus on survival needs. They accepted their situations without succumbing to them. Higher expressions of life spontaneously broke through even as their basic survival needs disappeared.

Letting Go ... Letting Go ...

For these creative choice makers, the actual turning point for this shift in perspective often occurred *after* the doctors shuttered the last ray of hope. Finally, they truly grasped that they had but a short time to live. Yet strikingly, these worst-case scenarios seemed to evoke the deepest personal growth.

For some of these people, basic survival needs disappeared one by one; for others, all at once. Many could not care for themselves, feed themselves, or even move their bodies. But having reached a point of utmost extremity where darkness seemed to overtake them completely, they allowed themselves to release their lives into the void without succumbing.

From this vantage of profound surrender, these transformers were able to view the world afresh. They conceived new desires and acted with what few abilities remained to them. As a consequence, their experience of life became greatly enhanced. Their inner declaration for "self," regardless of external circumstances, increasingly determined their sense of worth. Vitality bubbled through their everyday activities even as their abilities were stripped away.

Somehow, in dropping the need to keep intact the lower levels of survival and safety, they found themselves operating from a higher level of well-being.

When Do We Reach That Shift Point?

The depths to which we take a crisis before letting go to the Creation Cycle seem to be up to us. Every person I interviewed stated that it was the *letting go of their attachment to the problem or fear or judgment that freed them*, whether it was cancer or AIDS, a broken neck or a broken marriage, a lost home or job. Or all of the above and more.

No matter what our circumstances, our level of crisis and suffering is dependent on our attachment to an identity or belief. At some level, we choose to attach ourselves to certain concepts and ideals. We can also choose to let them go and embrace new ones. In the process, we experience that the quality of our lives changes dramatically.

The stories of Vivienne, Jeff, Joan, and Evy, as well as the testimonies of scores of other choice makers, all reveal that higher expressions of living are available to each of us *by choice*, even when we are confined by severe injury to a wheelchair or dying of an incurable illness. Before new creations coalesce from our chaos and confusion, the process requires letting go ... utterly.

The critical difference between highly creative acts and painful problems turns on a simple matter of perspective stated so succinctly by Shakespeare, *There is nothing either good or bad but thinking makes it so.* It's our perspective on it that makes the critical difference. From there, it all comes down to a choice of attitude, content of thought, and action.

The Creation Cycle Writ Large

It's fascinating that the three stages of crisis, chaos, and new creations are mirrored by cultures throughout the world in rites of passage from youth to adult. Spiritual initiations are found worldwide, from indigenous cultures throughout Africa to Aboriginal walkabouts in Australia, Native American vision quests, and Christian sacramental rites of passage.

All of these rituals are designed to challenge existing beliefs and behaviors, to change things up, and to reveal new truths that are accessible only from a fresh, more expansive perspective.

Looking back in history, we can see the Catholic Reformation, scientific revolution, and universal suffrage movement as distinct events that shaped the very reality we now use as a lens to frame our cultural identity. These events took on coherence as revolutions in new ways of thinking only after the fact. In the beginning stages, each of these periods of upheaval did not present any discrete new vision, but rather mounting discontent tearing apart the existing reality. This turmoil gradually fragmented existing cultural boundaries into chaos until wholly new and more powerful integrative forms slowly emerged and took root.

Today we seem to be undergoing a similar transitional period as we face an array of cultural challenges that may entrain profound shifts in our working beliefs. In each case, the outcome will depend on whether we collectively choose to open to a continually deepening integrative truth.

Chapter 5
Who Is the Chooser?

For in every case, man retains the freedom
and the possibility of deciding for or against
the influence of his surroundings.

— *Viktor Frankl, Holocaust survivor* —

To appreciate the profound growth that some experience through crisis, we need to seek the keys illuminating how our individual choice ignites the Creation Cycle. For some, as we have seen, such intentional choice in the face of crisis opens them to expanded states of being, regardless of physical circumstances.

Just so, the unbidden dance with chaos—the breakup of existing realities and resettling into the new—presents each of us with the opportunity to *consciously* make a difference in our own life course.

To invoke an old metaphor: Our life can be said to resemble a river flowing through time. We can look back to its beginnings and see the major forces shaping it into times of quiet stillness or tossing it into tumultuous rapids and out again. When floating down a river, we cannot see beyond the next bend, nor in the long view can we peer past the marshy deltas of old age. And we can only speculate what may become of us at the end of our journey once we merge with the seas of formless time from which we sprang.

While we're here, what we call "normal" is much like the map squiggle of a river, defining and giving shape to a concept: river. By contrast, crisis tears apart the very valley containing and directing our life flow. Job, marriage, home, family members, one's health—all can be lost in an instant, washed away in the flooding chaos.

Unlike a river, however, we humans possess choice and volition to gain new skills to better navigate the currents of life, or even carve new channels of expression. We also possess the choice to adhere to the past, confining our thoughts and actions to valleys already mapped by ourselves or others.

Holding Tight to Our Map

What we each believe as being real, of course, differs markedly between peoples, cultures, and historical ages. Once, the earth was the center of the universe. Once, magical fantasies of flying through the skies soared from the realm of dreams into everyday events. Today, women hide their faces in one country; in another they bare their bodies freely with pride. Ten thousand gods govern all facets of life in one corner of the world while governmental juntas reign in another.

Our beliefs surrounding what we consider real can run so deep that they may cause us to risk the alienation of others. We may even feel compelled to kill or die to defend them.

We hold on so hard to what we know. What else is there? No wonder it takes a crisis to bring us up short and challenge what we accept as true! Little do we recognize that the very act of holding on to our outmoded beliefs, our frozen identities, is what actually creates the discomfort of change. Resistance itself can turn the pain of a crisis into long-term suffering.

At the point Evy's doctor told her she was dying from incurable ALS and had one year to live, she fully accepted her fate. But in her desire to have "the best death," she inadvertently launched herself on a journey of discovery. Because she had never known self-love, her search for the keys unlocking that experience of love resulted in a radical perceptual shift.

I became what I call server—serving others from my wheelchair. What I saw was a world where there was a lot of things I could do. What I saw was a world not going to "hell in a hand basket." What I saw was a world I could contribute to, just as I was. And I was willing at that time to take a chance—with truth, love, joy, peace—because the other had not worked. So why not? I decided I didn't have anything to lose, and what I gained was life. So I repeated a thought: "If I die right now, what grade would I give myself? How would I grade myself? What would I want my life to be about?"

With these questions, Evy engaged the Creation Cycle, channeling her thoughts into very different patterns from those she had so fiercely held and defended before. All without having to fix anything.

Evy's journey through crisis follows the same pattern of post-traumatic growth (PTG) seen in the stories of other choice makers who transformed the quality of their life by choosing to see and act from a perspective of ability rather than disability. Together they give us a glimpse of the powerful capacity we all possess to become the choice makers of our own lives, to shape the contours of our own life quality.

Inside the Bubble

We take for granted the miraculous fact that we humans are equipped with the capacity to directly experience the world through our five senses and to mentally shape meaning, values, and beliefs about our experiences.

Notice that wherever you are, your thoughts and experiences form the windows to the world about you. It's as if we each live within a bubble that constantly shapes itself according to what we become aware of in the moment.

Until you read these words, you likely were not thinking of freezers or frogs or fingernails, but now they've instantly appeared within your bubble of awareness, haven't they?

The range of our experience and scope of our thoughts are determined by what we perceive in any given moment. *What's not perceived remains hidden.* This level of perception could be called the *first-level awareness,* and it encompasses two categories: our experiences and our concepts.

How First-Level Awareness Emerges

Recent research on brain development and perception reveals that humans begin to limit their range of perception at a very early age. According to research conducted by Patricia Kuhl, PhD, a neuroscientist at the University of Washington, babies who are six months old can distinguish between a wide range of sounds but gradually lose the ability to distinguish certain phonemes that are not found within their culture.

For instance, by twelve months, a Japanese baby has lost its inborn ability to perceive the difference between the sounds "la" and "ra," a distinction not made in the Japanese language. The baby's brain is already forming filters and conceptual categories that distort its subsequent perception of what is actually occurring. Every culture creates its own filters.[7]

In the same way, our senses are constantly bombarded by stimuli, but only a fraction is perceived at any one time, and some will always be filtered out. What we do perceive is affected by our culture, past experience, beliefs, and level of awareness.

Grooving Our Perceptual Maps

Our minds "in-form" us—literally shaping our experiences into meaningful form by creating a conceptual picture of our in-the-moment reality. This picture then tells us what is possible, impossible, good, evil, successful, worthy, and so on. It clothes us in our personal identity, framing the range of acceptable beliefs and behaviors.

In fact, the mind will attempt to take *any* experience and conceptualize it—put it into a form that is understandable and can be reacted to. Unfortunately, this can lead us to see only a limited outcome or cause us to react to our mind's formulations, rather than see what is really happening.

For this reason, it has been very difficult for me to communicate the nature of the most powerful event of my own life, which occurred in 1997 when I was unconscious for twenty minutes during a grand mal seizure. (See Chapter 12, "Beyond the Edge of Life.") Even though I had no recollection of the events in my bedroom and the frantic activity around me while unconscious, I found myself having what has been described as a near-death experience (NDE), an experience wholly beyond description. The phenomenon simply does not fit easily into any accepted medical theory or category.

Consequently, the most impactful event of my entire life has gone unacknowledged by the teams of doctors treating me over the past decade. My attempts to communicate to caregivers the nature of my powerful experiences were universally interpreted within existing medical frameworks that effectively shunted the event into the category of illusion, or delusion.

"Thinking Makes It So"

Let me tell a simpler tale for now, as I sit here pondering what lies outside my field of perception. Idly glancing up from my computer and peering out of my window, I suddenly notice a billowing, dark gray cloud forcing its way into the blue backdrop behind the trees outside my office.

A storm is brewing! I feel happy because it will water the garden for me. A storm is brewing! I feel frustrated since I'd planned to take my kids fishing today. A storm is brewing! I feel wistful—

the clouds dancing overhead remind me of my childhood days when my parents and I would fashion lounge chairs and umbrellas out of towels and driftwood and sand at the beach. We'd hunt for outlandish animals swirling through the sky and then laugh and run for cover when the rains hit...

Thus storms are good, bad, or exciting, depending on the meanings I impose on the experience.

And if I were to look from yet another perspective, I might see the menacing clouds overhead as just an isolated cumulonimbus passing by. When I peer through other windows facing other directions and invite new perceptions, a cobalt-blue sky shines brightly into my office.

My own limited first-level awareness and my past experiences frame the meanings I place on my current circumstance.

So What Did I Miss?

Engrossed in my thoughts about clouds, sprinklers, and fishing, I hadn't been aware of something crawling up my leg. When finally the hair on my thigh tickled me enough to grab my attention, my mind reacted reflexively. I leapt to my feet, frantically slapping and rubbing my leg as images of spiders, bees, and ticks raced through my mind.

Once the adrenaline rush and rapid heart rate subsided, I wondered at the smashed inchworm staining my leg and how it had gotten so far up before I became aware of it. The experience had instantly triggered a response from my concepts, based upon fears and past experience, about *what is dangerous*, which then instantly determined my next actions.

Now I'm saddened, because I happen to like inchworms.

Our experiences constantly interact with our thoughts, giving meaning and value to any experience we have, which in turn helps us frame meaning for future experiences. This can be very useful. But often our beliefs become hardened by judgments or choreographed from learned behaviors that keep us traveling down very defined roads of thinking, emoting, and acting. Along the way, we may miss the play of life unfolding before us.

Shifting the Lens of Perception

In my work as a rehabilitation specialist, I found that many of my clients were not only saddled by significant disabilities but also overwhelmed by the stress of financial constraints, advanced age, limited education, and work history. From the perspective of their disability piled on top of myriad other problems—relationship issues, stress of kids, etc., desperately few options appeared to be available. They saw their cup as less than half-empty.

Unless they could shift perspective by choosing also to focus on their residual abilities and fresh desires, the future looked bleak indeed.

To help them experience the power of becoming their own *chooser* of perspective, I often situated my client to face away from the door of the office and look toward the back wall, so they were unable to see the window or door. I then posed a question: "How would you get out of the room in an emergency if your only options were limited to seeing very solid-looking walls surrounding you, framed by your current perspective?"

Without choosing any new viewpoint, each could easily convince themselves and a jury of their peers that going through walls would be extremely difficult and painful. No other possibilities existed. The doorway remained out of view.

This exercise proved very effective in helping people see that their fixed perspective on their problems kept them rooted in place.

One man, however, shocked me by exposing my own limited thinking. When he sat in the chair facing the back of the room and I posed the question of how he would get out without changing perspective, he responded without hesitation, "No problem! I'd climb on the table, pull up a chair to stand on, and go through the ceiling!"

Sure enough, as in many newer buildings, the office had a false hanging ceiling that accessed other parts of the building.

This power of pulling back and observing our own concepts and experiences is immense, since it opens us to an infinite domain of creative potential. By being the chooser of perspective, we can, at any moment, turn to face the same circumstance from a new direction, inviting previously unseen doorways of opportunity to swing open.

Or, maybe we go through the ceiling.

The Emotional Mind Field

Emotions comprise both domains of concepts and experiences: Sensory input endowed with a quality or meaning becomes one of the most powerful drivers of human action taken from first-level awareness. Linking a meaning to sensory feelings can ignite passions which forge actions and reactions, ripping apart the very things we seek to fulfill us.

If anything is capable of leading us around like a bull on a nose ring, it's our emotions. Just swing by any sports arena on a busy Saturday or Sunday during a hotly contested game. Or read the occasional reports of the fights breaking out where we learn about a guy's ear bitten clean off or fans trampled to death. And that's only a game!

Think of the power of emotion unleashed in a highly charged political debate or religious confrontation. Or emotions unleashed in the wake of a lost loved one. Or when the doctor gently breaks the news of a terminal diagnosis.

We readily see how people undergoing the exact same experience can snap into opposing action based upon their preset beliefs. My family lives near a naval air base, and fighter jets often fly in close formation right over our house, rattling the windows and setting the ground trembling in their wake. I watch my neighbor on one side of us scowling at the jet noise, cussing at the pork barrel politics and bureaucratic controls the noise signifies to him. My neighbor on the other side salutes with patriotic fervor, believing himself more safe and secure by their presence.

Both believe they are right about the truth of jet planes and naval bases and governmental roles and how they improve—or diminish—their personal quality of life.

Tango from Second-Level Awareness

But there is a way not to be trapped within the limits of concepts and emotions that we stamp upon all of our experiences. Another domain is available that opens us to unlimited possibilities—*one that brings the opportunity of observation, or awareness, of our thoughts, experiences, and emotions.* This domain has been called second-level awareness. To keep things simple, I refer to it as "awareness"—the level from which choice makers act.

Once we are aware of an experience, concept, or emotion, we can freely choose our response, rather than react from our old programming. Awareness of our experiences and thoughts offers us the ability to *choose a response* to any situation, to tango rather than duel.

Let's revisit my warring neighbors. Because of their different reactions to the sound of jet planes flying overhead, my neighbors don't speak to one another. Both share the same experience, but their personal conceptual frameworks produce very different realities.

Imagine if they were to observe their own inner contradictions (conscious awareness) and notice how their reactions were being driven by their concepts and emotions. A whole array of new choices could emerge for achieving what each was really striving for personally and within their relationship: communication.

Like my neighbors who react viscerally when the other's name is mentioned, we each limit our ability to respond by reacting from set beliefs and emotions—from first-level awareness. In the heat of a moment, have you done or said anything you later regretted? Ever felt frozen in place from fear? Or maybe felt dragged into a pit of depression or malaise to the point you didn't even feel like getting out of bed?

Rational action is typically seen as a higher level of expression than an emotional response. But as we've noted, the rational domain cannot embrace more than concepts, and concepts cannot fully embrace the experience of love or happiness, or for that matter, encompass depression or terror. To choose from conscious awareness is to choose how we engage our thoughts, experiences, and emotions.

Rationality is always tied to a particular conceptual framework. Once aware of the framework itself, we have the power to choose to change it. A new one wraps an experience into an entirely different meaning, causing the most rational of responses to change like a chameleon.

The practice of being aware of our thoughts, emotions, and experiences opens us to the possibility of an unbounded presence of peace and wholeness, no matter how adverse our circumstances.

Choice When There Is No Choice

Without seeing the possibility of choice, human will crumples. When peoples' identity, value, and purpose waste away, they often sink into helplessness, unwilling to take action in their own behalf. No one understood this better than Viktor Frankl, the renowned psychiatrist and humanist who survived the concentration camps at Auschwitz and Türkheim during World War II.

At first, Dr. Frankl lived in the hope of being reunited with his family. But after learning of the deaths of both his wife and parents in the camps, he became suicidal. At that point, he happened upon some scraps of paper on which he'd roughed out portions of an early book he called *Doctor of the Soul.* He vowed that he would at least finish the book before killing himself.

Instead, writing the book filled him with renewed energy and purpose.

In the midst of all the horror, grief, and degradation, Frankl came to grasp that his freedom to choose his perspective would be the key to his own survival and sanity. Daily he faced choices about how to respond to the torture, starvation, and wholesale slaughter of humanity around him.

> *In every case, man retains the freedom and the possibility of deciding for or against the influence of his surroundings. Although he may seldom exert this freedom or use this opportunity to choose—it is open for him to do so.* [8]

Who better than Viktor Frankl to claim this insight?

Becoming Conscious Choice Makers

Once crisis cracks open the shell of what we see as reality and our world falls apart, what's left? Awareness—if we claim it.

Awareness of what has been lost but also of what remains. Awareness of what we are thinking and emoting in this moment. Awareness of the choices we can make to shape the perspectives giving our lives purpose and meaning every day.

If we're acting from awareness of our thoughts and experiences (second-level), we now have the power to choose our response to whatever we are aware of, including the content of our own beliefs.

Each choice maker whose story illuminates these pages has made the shift from a problem-centered to a creative-centered perspective. Each chooses to see abundant ability and creative potential just as they are, and to frame problems within the context of a larger whole where new choices constantly reveal themselves.

PTG and Maslow

Psychologist Abraham Maslow was one of the first of his contemporaries to map the natural tendency of humans to strive toward growth. He devised the Hierarchy of Needs in 1943, forming an important element of his widely recognized theory of human motivation.

Dr. Maslow observed that once people's basic survival needs are met and their security and self-esteem safeguarded, they naturally strive toward filling higher needs of justice, beauty, and internal qualities of self-actualization. Stress and other adverse forces tend to limit or even push down the level of well-being, so that people do not always operate from the same levels consistently.

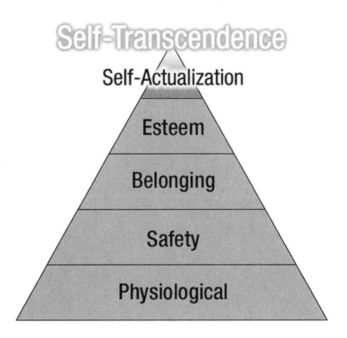

Figure 2. Maslow's Hierarchy of Needs, including the later addition of a sixth level he termed "Self-Transcendence."

The Hierarchy of Needs ascends from the lowest level—meeting basic survival needs—to activating the highest ideals of human fulfillment in self-actualization and transcendence, with each higher-level need assumed to emerge from the fulfillment of a lower-level need below it.

Here's where we encounter an intriguing developmental dilemma. Maslow's description of those qualities found in self-actualized people bear a remarkable resemblance to the outcomes we've seen in those who grow or transform through crisis. Paradoxically, however, post-traumatic growth research shows consistently that people open to the higher levels on Maslow's scale as a *consequence* of crisis when their very foundation of survival and self-identity is actually under threat or even destroyed.

Maslow himself came to recognize this inherent weakness in his model. He too observed people whose safety and survival needs were not being met, but who exhibited the higher motivation he ascribed to self-actualization. As his own thinking evolved, he rectified this problem at least in part by developing the concept of self-transcendence. (Most texts even today describe only the first five levels of Maslow's hierarchy, which he amended in the 1960s.)

Climbing Maslow's Pyramid by Choice Alone

Conscious choice makers open to the highest states represented by Maslow's model despite being totally bereft of basic assurances of their own safety and security. Often, in fact, permanent disruptions have changed the course of their lives, or they are dying. By choice, these individuals let go of identification with loss and their past to naturally embrace the attributes identified at the higher levels of the pyramid. The similarities between Maslow's conceptions of self-actualized people and the traits of thrivers who evince PTG are unmistakable:

- Accepting themselves and their own natures.
- Pursuing continued development and continued growth.
- Enjoying a deepening sense of appreciation.
- Embodying a deep kinship with others.
- Seeing beyond differences to underlying causes and connections.
- Embracing ethical and moral actions naturally.

Even though many texts continue to treat Maslow's five-stage model as a complete theory, the importance of his addition of self-transcendence cannot be overstated. In 2006, an article published in the journal *Review of General Psychology* examined both Maslow's published and unpublished works and concluded that Maslow "places the highest form of human development at a transpersonal level, where the self/ego and its needs are transcended. This represents a monumental shift in the conceptualization of human personality and its development."[9]

Incorporating Maslow's conception of transcendence would open the way to embracing a more comprehensive understanding of the "underpinnings of altruistic behaviors, social progress, and wisdom."[10]

Expanding the Circle

As we have seen, choice reveals itself in the light of awareness—and this expanded awareness multiplies the range of choices available to us in any moment. The Circle of Perception in Figure 3 on the next page illustrates how we are free to choose to expand our perceived options by identifying with an ever-larger whole and aligning our thoughts and actions accordingly. If our awareness focuses on survival and individual needs, then fighting others for the best advantage is only natural. By expanding awareness to include the well-being of others, we not only secure our own survival needs but do so in ways that actively serve the world around us.

Figure 3. Expanding our Circle of Perception. From awareness, we are free to choose our level of perspective, from focusing on basic self-needs to growth and self-actualization. Awareness infuses yet transcends all levels.

Notice that no matter what we think or experience, we retain the capacity to be aware of our thoughts and experience unbounded by any circumstance—what Maslow labeled self-transcendence. Scope of perception, not limitation in circumstance, determines the range of possible choices before us.

To illustrate again with Evy's story: Once Evy set out to discover what constituted love and acceptance before she died—a creative stance—she began to respond to herself and others from a much more expansive level, one that encompassed compassion and forgiveness even as her body remained incapacitated. In her telling, she was able to truly love for the first time.

Let's see how realization of the power to choose the level of perspective played out for my sister-in-law Laurie.

Laurie's Story

Since she was diagnosed with breast cancer in 2005, Laurie has come to see her world from a new and expanded vantage. To start with, she told me how she got past her fears:

> *I learned that I needed to stop being consumed by cancer fears and move on to other things. I had a lot of living to do and just needed to find a meaningful way to spend my time. Obsessing about what could be was not it. I saw how much my friends liked me and how sad they'd be if I were gone. I didn't want sadness, as my life has been good and productive—something that's important to me.*
>
> *I also learned not to fear death, as it can be peaceful and beautiful. A day worrying is a day not living.*

I asked her why she thought some people faced with crises like hers, Joan's, or Vivienne's thrived when others folded. Laurie thought about this for a moment and then made a very important observation—that cancer had forced her to explore what was important.

> *Before cancer, I was a planner, never really present in my body. As I was doing "the thing" I'd just planned, I was busy planning the next thing. Yikes! I now realize the futility of this.*

Laurie has thought a lot about why she had to face her ordeal of illness and recovery. She pondered whether she "got cancer" rather than some other malady because it would take away her pressing sense of future—thus forcing her to change her pattern of hurrying on to the next thing.

She has also deeply pondered the question of some sort of higher power at play and commented that, if this were the case, it would imply a divine plan whereby one's disease or accident might function to bring insight.

> *It's interesting to contemplate. Was it just random chance that I got cancer and it gave me wisdom in one of many areas that needed work? I have no idea, but I am grateful for the new wisdom that it has brought to me.*

Laurie's path to a more expanded state of being, like that of so many choice makers, came at a very high price. Why did she not fold during her long trial?

> *I haven't a clue. Maybe it was that being scared and sad was just no fun and I made the conscious choice to be happy. Is it this simple?*

Indeed, is it?

It seems the challenge lies in our willingness to choose *consciously*, and that willingness blossoms *in its own season* from our journey through the jungles of pain, grief, and loss.

Choice Makers Tool Kit—Short Version

To summarize, common to all choice makers are a number of fundamental choices:

- *Accept* what is—all of it.
- *Own* your feelings—anger, fear, frustration, and so on— as yours.
- *Express* emotions safely—all of them.

- *Focus* on residual ability within the loss and disability.
- *Act* on seeds of desire to create for yourself and others.
- *Share* yourself. Reach out to be of service to others.
- *Let go* of results. You are here just now. Be in the experience, fully.

Remember, choice is always available in the moment. Just now, for instance, you can choose to find something to appreciate—a color's hue, a cobweb's intricacy, a comedy's lightness, the ability to breathe. It may be whisked away by the problems or emotions swirling about you in the next moment, but when aware, you can rechoose.

Caveat

Although it may sound as if choice makers make a single momentous decision to opt for expanded options, in practice they often proceed by a one-step-forward, half-step-back kind of dynamic. For some, the process might entail years of slow transformation. Finally, the realization dawns that growth contains no end point.

For myself, I've found that a simple, ten-minute daily practice of expanding my Circle of Perception—opening new and novel choices to respond to what's happening in my life—makes a huge difference in my well-being. By setting my intention to let go of past limitations and be open to new possibilities and solutions, powerful dynamics come into play that, over time, change my attitudes and actions in ways I couldn't have foreseen.

Are You Taking a Creative Stance?

Following is a brief checklist to test your own set of attitudes and stances to the problems and challenges your life currently presents.

Are you willing to:

- Open to and accept what is happening *just now*?
- Expand your Circle of Perception by peering beyond the edge of old structures and beliefs and open to new ways of seeing your world?
- Allow a range of emotional states to emerge and subside without getting trapped within them? (The expression of emotions allows one's suppressed feelings to emerge—denial, anger, depression, defeat—which can be expressed safely and without harm to others.)
- Take direct action and focus on what can be done now with whatever abilities or resources that are already available to you?
- Drop attachment to seeming limitations imposed by the problem?
- Step back, see yourself as whole and complete—just this present moment ... and again this moment?

If so, you're ready to check your habitual mode of expression against *words that keep you stuck* and *words that create*.

Words To Stay Stuck In or Words To Create By

We can observe which type of perspective we're using—problem-oriented versus creative-oriented—by listening to our own words. Read through the first series of statements ("Words To Stay Stuck In") on the following page. Then contrast them with "Words To Create By" on page 79. Which do you tend to practice?

Words To Stay STUCK In

Problem-centered statements:

- My problem is…
- I've already tried…
- You just don't understand…
- It can't be done. I can prove it.
- I don't have enough money (help, time, support, health, education)…
- If only things were better—my parents (job, spouse, bank account)…

Dual statement of ability/disability finds a way it won't work:

- Of course I want to succeed, but…
- *I'm* willing, but *they* screwed it up…
- Of course I want to, but it's not possible…
- I can see how others can succeed, but they don't have *my* problem.

Reinterpreting other people's statements to raise barriers:

- They won't let me.
- They (fill in the blank) have the power and money, and won't listen to me.
- My teacher (parent, boss) told me I was not good enough, smart enough…
- The doctor (other authority) will not let me do it.
- No one understands the real issues.

Words To CREATE By

Action-oriented statements:

- I desire ... (a creative impulse)
- I am able ...
- I choose to ...
- I am taking this step ...

Dual statement acknowledging problem, but seeing possibility beyond its edge:

- I can't fix my problem (i.e., get out of my wheel-chair), but *I can* ...
- I am experiencing pain (fear, loss), *and yet I am able to* ...
- The doctors gave me a month to live. *Still, I'm alive today and have the ability to* ...
- I can fully grieve my loss (child, spouse, job, house) while being open to how the loss can deepen my own life experience.

When confronted by obstacles, I can ask:

- How can I see this differently?
- What might the obstacles be calling to my attention?
- If I could remove the obstacles, am I clear about what I really want to create?
- If I got what I'm wanting, what would I experience?
- What action *can* I take just now to bring that experience alive?

Dr. Gartman's Surprise—A Story from My Own Life

I can personally attest to the power of the Creation Cycle, especially the power of following a clear intention with focused action, then letting go of the results to allow all possible options—including failure.

When I was born, the doctors discovered a birth defect in my aortic heart valve. As I grew, I found myself becoming Exhibit A for a parade of physicians and interns making detours to listen to the weird sound of this kid's heart. When I reached my teenage years, my body outgrew the capacity of my heart to feed it oxygen during high exertion, and I began for the first time to feel the direct effects of limited blood flow.

I adjusted, and although I could not run for more than a few seconds before exhausting the oxygen stored in my body, I found I could maintain an aerobic state when climbing and hiking. But by my early twenties, my heart problems increased, eliminating even mild exercise. Finally I underwent open-heart surgery at age twenty-five to implant a newly invented mechanical aortic valve.

Although it proved rather noisy to my loved ones, the artificial valve opened the door to my climbing mountains again, taking me up 14,410-foot Mount Rainier and on many other glorious adventures. The artificial valve lasted thirty years.

When in 2005 I faced the prospect of a second open-heart surgery, I searched for the best surgeon around. After interviewing several, I finally settled on Dr. David Gartman, a protégé of my first surgeon, Dr. Dillard.

What had really grabbed my attention was an off-hand comment he made during our initial meeting. "I feel my own intention plays an important role in my success. It seems silly, but I had a remarkable insight one day while watching a B-action movie about a superhero who would get trapped in these impossible situations. Every time the hero ran out of options and the bad guys were closing in, he'd say to himself, 'I am the best! I am the best!' "

Dr. Gartman smiled a little self-consciously. "It may seem a bit arrogant, but I saw the value in taking that kind of stand, and I choose to see myself as the best. I found taking that stand has really helped me in tight spots when I'm confronting what seems to be an impossible situation."

Dr. Gartman's ability to step back to observe, and his willingness to stand in the face of the unknown and hold a space open for unseen possibilities, made him my choice of surgeon.

A few weeks later, after both my boys promised to climb the glaciers on Mount Baker with me once I recovered, I entered the hospital for my second open-heart surgery. I held a clear intention as I watched the anesthetic being injected into my veins— my focus was on fulfilling my promise to my sons.

As I chatted with my wife and the anesthesiologist, I knew the doctors literally held my life in their hands. My last memory was describing my research regarding the effects of consciousness on physical healing. (Once I became unconscious, I imagine they all had a good laugh about it.)

After a protracted surgery, I was finally wheeled into the recovery room. The next morning, I groggily came to enough to recognize Dr. Gartman standing by my bed, who asked how I was doing. My slow, stuttered response elicited silence, and then a long stare. Evidently, I'd mumbled something about feeling like I'd been driven over by a tractor.

He gave me a long look, finally saying softly, "It's a good day to be alive." He lingered a moment more, his hand on the bed rail, then slowly turned away.

Several days later, when I was still in the hospital and after unexpected complications subsided, my wife asked Dr. Gartman why the surgery had taken so long. He explained, "Once I took out the old mechanical valve and cut away all the damage it caused to the aortic arch over the last thirty years, only a mass of shreds remained. I didn't see how it could possibly be repaired. There literally was nothing to put together again."

No matter how he tried, he could find no way to reconstruct the complex aortic arch. Finally, not seeing any way to proceed, he stepped back from the operating table, and for five full minutes closed his eyes as he mentally flipped through three-dimensional images of the heart, valve seat, and aortic arch.

All the while, the rest of the surgical team looked on in puzzlement, wondering at his long silence and impassive stance.

Finally, he saw a possibility and took action.

My wife asked, "What would have happened if you couldn't have found a way to repair it?"

Dr. Gartman answered simply, "Some people don't ever get off the table, you know."

Chapter 6
Supporting Others

At times our own light goes out
and is rekindled by a spark from another person.
Each of us has cause to think with deep gratitude
of those who have lighted the flame within us.

— *Albert Schweitzer* —

One intriguing element that keeps popping up in these stories of letting go to chaos is the role of support. We can see how crisis can act as catalysts for transformation, but how can we support our friends and loved ones in the transformational process?

Some crises irreparably shatter the known. People, institutions, and whole nations succumb to intractable problems, trapping them in lingering limitation and suffering, or even deterioration toward death. Others transform. This much seems obvious to the researchers of post-traumatic growth, who have demonstrated that catastrophic trauma may have a positive impact on self, life philosophy, and relationships. However, the research models do not provide any predictive power to help differentiate between those who succumb or those who transform.

These researchers have assumed that an important determinant of growth after crisis is the level of family and social support surrounding the person moving through trauma. But in fact, an extensive review of the research by graduate student Christine Pierce reports that the level of social support provided by friends, family, or intimate relationships was *not* significant in promoting PTG. [11] This leaves us with the question: Is there a type of support that *is* a significant factor in promoting growth?

What Makes for Effective Support?

During those times I've felt lost or been caught in a web of intractable problems of failing health, financial loss, or unhappy relationships, I noticed a distinct difference in the type of support others offered me and how useful it was. And based on my work with hundreds of injured workers I counseled during my twenty-five years as a rehabilitation professional, it became clear that the *type and timing* of support proffered is critical to its effectiveness.

Providing initial support to someone in crisis obviously centers on stopping the bleeding and repairing damage. There is an initial marshaling of resources to physically and emotionally support effective treatment. After that, we bring comfort and chicken soup, give reassurance, and often serve as an advocate for our friend or family member. And, of course, don't forget the flowers!

But as we've seen, the path toward PTG leads beyond just repairing the past or soothing present hurts and requires the person in crisis to take an active role in readjusting to a different world. Supporting that person through the chaos and creation stages requires a different relationship between him or her, and us. Individuals in crisis require time and space to grieve losses and fully let go of the past, move through the wilderness of chaos and limbo, and actively pursue a future of their own choosing.

Beggar's Opera

Early one morning, as I pondered why the immense resources available through medical and rehabilitation services often founder, I happened to catch this story on my kitchen radio...

> *After leaving the Marines, George Hill became addicted*
> *to drugs and alcohol. He soon found himself on the streets*
> *of Los Angeles, homeless for a dozen years.*
> *"I can't even begin to tell you the misery of rain," he*

says. *"I don't even care how slight the rainfall is, it was misery beyond belief.*

"Sometimes you sleep during the day because it's warm enough to sleep. And then at night you keep moving so you don't freeze.

"You would watch people get on buses and think, 'Those are normal people.' You felt anything but normal and I was just looking for a change," Hill says.

"I was sitting on a bag, and here comes a homeless man, so dirty it was just awful. His hands were black, with the exception of his knuckles and joints, where the bone had kind of rubbed through the dirt. He had rags tied on his feet. And his hair was matted in two big, nasty dreads.

"Out of all the people on skid row, he looked down at me and reached in his pocket and pulled out a dollar in change. It's all he had, and he gave it to me and said, 'Here, man. I feel sorry for you.' And he shuffled away."

Something about that moment changed everything for Hill.

"I just said, 'Oh, no, no … I'm going to get some help.' "

With the money the man gave him, Hill says he took a bus to a hospital psych unit.

"I still think about it sometimes," he says. *"I don't believe in trying to make up for lost time. And I don't have regrets for anything that happened, because going through the homelessness just made me so grateful, determined, thankful.*

"Now, every time it rains and I have keys in my pocket, I have a joy of life that you cannot believe."

Hill has now been off the streets for ten years. He has a job with the U.S. Department of Veterans Affairs and is pursuing a degree in computer information systems at Cal State University.[12]

Talk about support from an unexpected source! A homeless man occupying the bottom rung of society, powerless and dressed in rags and dirt, effectively cracked open George Hill's world by jolting his perspective. Once George committed to change and took action in his own behalf, the very systems that failed him before became effective allies in building his new life.

To more carefully determine the value of support, we need to understand why the type of support we give or receive is crucial.

Limits of Problem-Centered Support

Grappling with the problem is the traditional approach we humans use to conquer challenges to our survival and self-worth. To fix our problem and defend against new threats, we need to fortify protective barriers and marshal the resources to combat it.

In conformance with the "grappling principle," my job as a rehabilitation professional meant attempting to return injured workers to their previous levels of functioning. The focus, therefore, required me to define my clients' precrisis life and attempt to return them—using a finite set of resources—as close as possible to their previous level of ability and state of well-being.

Sometimes we succeed in reclaiming our precrisis normal, but oftentimes we cannot. Whether it be a wayward spouse, terminal illness, or lost job, the problem and its ready solution are obviously beyond our immediate control.

Similarly, our efforts as professional helpers are often doomed to fail when our client cannot be returned to a precrisis state. When all efforts aimed at eliminating the problem or providing the means to accommodate a loss founder, and the conditions become chronic, so does the perceived need for continued outside assistance. Our client has become dependent on system support.

This is the reason rehabilitation and social support systems often produce just the opposite of what they try so hard to achieve. Few stop to consider a wholly different approach, one that the next three chapters address in depth.

Needing a Friend to Set Her Straight

Evy, who once worked as the director of nursing at a major hospital, learned about what constitutes effective support the hard way. After a lifetime of struggling with the residual effects of polio and following her diagnosis of terminal ALS, she returned to work in a wheelchair. Most of her co-workers treated her the same as before. This infuriated her. But she also angrily rebuffed those who did acknowledge the change in her condition and tried to reach out to her.

Once she worked through her intense anger and resentment, Evy saw how she so strongly identified herself as disabled.

> *First I had polio, then poisoning, surgery, an accident, heart disease, and a car accident. I had something that I recovered from but each progressive incident got worse. My life had been one tragedy after another. The result? I got attention. I became the center of attention. I was special when I was ill. I did not feel special when I was not ill.*
>
> *When I was ill I was in control. My mother would spend hours with me in the hospital; my father would be there every chance he could. I was really controlling other people's lives. They were being run by me.*

Confronting her impending death head-on turned Evy's attention toward a new way of understanding what kind of support she needed.

> *It was at that point I made the conscious decision to stop the Ferris wheel I was on. I now examined how my life could be different. What could I do? A friend is one who*

would kick me in the ass. Sometimes it takes that to help
someone get off the Ferris wheel.

Ability-Centered Support

Supporting others as they move toward new creation without changing their immediate circumstances sometimes starts by our simply letting go of control, both inner and outer. For example, cancer patient Claire was bravely weathering painful chemotherapy and attempting to keep her spirits up by using affirmations of healing and focusing entirely on positive thoughts. Her friends kept close watch on her and tried to support her positive attitude throughout her ordeal.

One day, during their weekly lunch together in a busy restaurant, Claire broke down in uncontrollable sobbing. Unable to console her, her friends could only stand by helplessly and witness her outpouring of grief.

Later, however, she told them her breakdown was a major turning point for her:

When I let myself express what I really felt inside, I discovered my courage. No longer do I hold back feelings.
That includes the pain and depression, but also the joy I lost somewhere along the way in all the fear and struggling and holding things "together."

What Helped Jeff Put the Creation Cycle in Play?

After Jeff broke his neck playing football, support from others was critical in helping him accept his inability to perform even the simplest tasks he once took for granted—and to refocus on new challenges and abilities. When asked what best supported him, Jeff responded without hesitation:

Well, my mom helped me a lot. I would pose her with my dilemmas and problems. My mom is really good at gadgets and figuring something out or finding someone to figure something out to help me. If I posed a problem to her, she would be able to take it and work with it. She knew what I had and what I didn't have physically, so we would basically brainstorm and find a way to do it. When I left the hospital, they gave me a splint to put on my hand to help me hold things. Well, I didn't want to do anything that would draw attention to my disability other than my chair, so I refused to wear the splint. I learned that I could, just by trial and error, use a felt-tip pen because it didn't require any pressure to write with. It was just a matter of learning to write down key words because I'm not a very fast writer. Exercising my mental ability to recall once I write something down helped me to trigger other thoughts related to the notes.

The neighborhood I grew up in supported me in so many ways. My brothers, my friends, and my brother's friends were all very helpful. Since I couldn't do sports, I got involved in the student body as a way to keep engaged with other students. I found I needed to raise my grades in order to run for student government. I think that's when I first learned I was going to have to start depending on my brain instead of my physical attributes.

Accepting Help from Within and Without

The role of crisis involves both a time of being supported by others and a time of allowing the inner self to seek out new perspectives and opportunities. Understanding this two-part process can help us intervene more effectively and assist others to turn their attention, *and intention*, toward change and growth.

Supporting growth through crisis significantly differs from the stance of crisis management, which directly attempts to fix the problem and reclaim the precrisis state we call "normal." We can become more adept at harnessing the power of crisis as a transformational agent. By no longer focusing only on efforts to stamp it out, we can begin to see latent opportunities inherent within the crisis itself.

We can also see how to better support a person through the chaotic period of letting go and before the crystallization of new creations. Offering empowered support changes the context of crisis, opening a person to new possibilities unseen in the preoccupation with problems.

How to Support the Creation Cycle

Crisis: The focus is on survival, triage, treatment, succor, and solutions. We help ourselves and others by seeking effective aid to mitigate the trauma and in acknowledging and grieving the loss.

Chaos: As choice makers, we radically let go of both past and future and acknowledge the truth of what's happening in this very moment. It's a time of stepping back to experiment with new perspectives and new possibilities.

Creation: We now choose to see opportunity and ability within ourselves and others. Take active steps, just as we are, toward new creations aligned with our deepest desires.

Kristin's Story

Not so long ago, I saw first-hand the power of supporting a renewal track that invited open-ended creations. My son Eron and his girlfriend Kristin were in an auto accident that smashed in her side of the car all the way to the midline. Without prompt aid, Kristin would have died from her injuries. She was immediately flown to the regional trauma center and remained in a coma for five days.

Medical personnel flowed in and out of Kristin's room, and family members remained by her side twenty-four hours a day. Obviously, intense grief overwhelmed everyone at times. Fresh emotions erupted over each new diagnostic test revealing a damaged spleen, liver, fractured ribs, and collarbone; a possible broken neck; and severe brain trauma.

During the first twelve hours after the accident, decisions about surgery to Kristin's spleen and liver were made and delayed, while the doctors simultaneously ran a battery of tests to determine the extent of damage to her neck and brain. The fractured ribs, collarbone, and three fractures to her lower spine seemed trivial in comparison to the life-threatening problems.

As Kristin was stabilized over the first thirty-six hours, something remarkable occurred. We two families began to see and engage with her in a different way. Without discussion, over the course of those first days after the accident, we evolved a whole new way of seeing her and responding to her. It could be passed off as primarily a coping strategy, but the families' change also happened to be the most powerful way of truly supporting Kristin. How did it come about?

The Power of Family Unity

The foundation for this change rested on the cohesiveness of both families. My son Eron had been the driver, Kristin the passenger. Yet no acrimony or blame, victimization, or finger pointing ever erupted between any of the parties. Rather, we all became like one close-knit, extended family, focused only on Kristin's well-being. Whenever tests confirmed a problem, the family adjusted to face the challenge and to find a way forward. Nothing was denied or hidden from open discussion.

Every little change over the next several days was celebrated. When Kristin's eyes teared slightly in the presence of her loved ones, the waiting room erupted at the news, celebrating as if witnessing a long-awaited birth.

Other signs followed: Eron, who stood vigil by her bedside day and night, late one evening felt a slight squeeze of her hand. Kristin's mother also took up permanent residence in the intensive care unit and was thrilled when Kristin finally responded to her voice by turning her head slightly.

Any sign of consciousness, however minuscule, was immediately relayed to the waiting room, texted, e-mailed, blogged, and telephoned to family, friends, school, and the whole community faster than Paul Revere could saddle up his horse.

Staff Help Empower Kristin's Recovery

Without exception, the hospital staff elegantly supported an ability-based intervention. The doctors clearly stated to the family the facts of Kristin's state: the diagnoses, the unknowns, the alternatives, and the decisions needed. They clearly laid out the challenges, but not once did I hear the staff impose a limitation upon Kristin's future.

Instead, their words impeccably mirrored the doctors' stance of seeing open-ended potential while still remaining clear about her present condition.

As they entered the room, each member of the staff addressed the comatose Kristin directly, telling her exactly what procedures they were going to do, talking to her while they performed them, and conversing with her about the next steps and how well she was doing as they left.

To the casual observer, the friendly conversational tone the doctors, therapists, and nurses were taking toward an immobile, totally unconscious and unresponsive body might seem a bit extreme, or nonsensical. But the atmosphere they created was one of honoring Kristin's presence and coaxing her participation as essential to discovering her status, planning her treatment to help in determining the best next steps.

Kristin Collaborates Despite Her Coma

Staff effectively engaged family members as participants and fellow collaborators rather than the deciders of Kristin's fate. By talking to her directly, it was as if she were the one collaborating with *them* to develop her treatment. They tacitly acknowledged Kristin as an active partner, who owned the ability to be an active participant in her own healing.

It's unknown how much, if any, of their conversation Kristin actually heard while in the coma. But their "dialogue" with Kristin very effectively kept everyone's attention on her ability to act in the midst of what otherwise could have been seen as the overwhelming crisis of a broken life.

Kristin's mother and Eron acted as her eyes and ears, describing for her the bustle of activity swirling around her room. They were especially helpful when Kristin began to jerk spasmodically, sometimes pulling out her life-giving tubes and intravenous needles. They would stand on either side of her, talking to her, gently guiding her arms to guard against her hurting herself.

Over a period of a day and a half, I watched Eron teach Kristin not to tear out her tubes in reaction to the skin irritation the tubes and tape caused her. With infinite patience, he helped her learn to scratch around the layers of tape irritating her nose, rather than reflexively ripping off the tape or pulling out the feeding tube threaded through her nostril.

Kristin also learned to stay away from the other critical life support lines well before we saw any overt signs of her being aware of her surroundings. Without constant attendance by Eron and Kristin's mother, she would have required restraint by strapping her arms and legs to the bed, which is common protocol for unconscious patients.

Kristin's Friends in Shock

After Kristin's vital signs stabilized sufficiently, her friends from school were allowed to visit, even though she remained in a deep coma and was still intubated. One afternoon, two friends from school stopped by. What they saw sent them both into shock. Frozen in place, speechless, they stared at Kristin's inert body festooned by its tubes and monitors, and without uttering a word, turned about and left, both obviously shaken.

Kristin's friends held only a perspective of the Kristin they knew before the accident: the vivacious soccer player, gymnast, and cheerleader. What they now saw was a Kristin unable to move, talk, open her eyes, or acknowledge them in any way.

After seeing the glazed look in their eyes, my wife followed them back out to the waiting room to help them come to grips with what they had witnessed.

By the fourth day, as I watched yet another set of ashen-faced friends stumble out of the room, I realized how radically different our families' approach to Kristin had been and how it might be affecting her recovery. We continuously looked for signs of her progress, ability, and change, whether it was a monitor removed, her vitals stabilizing, or a flicker of response in her fingers or eyelids.

Staying Positive Despite the Strain

Of course, in the hallways or in private, the red eyes of each family member bore evidence of the grief and fear of possibly never again seeing the Kristin we knew before calamity struck. Temporary denial, prayers, and hope helped to soften bad news. When the doctors stated that she might require surgery on her liver and spleen, we rallied around their statement that, since she was young and in good physical condition before the accident, she would be able to handle whatever might come her way.

But no one let fear run the show, and no one, including the doctors and nurses, placed any kind of shadow over her potential healing by citing statistics or verbally defining their beliefs about her ultimate limitations.

Dramatic Change

More than two weeks after the accident, she was making remarkable gains. Still unable to talk or focus her eyes, Kristin stared right through visitors as if they didn't exist.

One morning I watched Eron and Kristin sit side-by-side "pretexting" each other. Because Kristin remained mute and unable even to make a sound, she and Eron communicated by writing notes to each other on a white board—one would write or draw a message, the other would respond, then erase the board and start over. Maybe primitive text messaging, but effective, and cute.

We looked forward to the day the speech pathologist would start therapy to prepare the way for Kristin to learn to swallow or intentionally cough on command. These, we were told, would be the initial stages of her regaining control of her vocal cords, which were expected to take several months before she would likely talk again.

All that changed suddenly when, just before breakfast, the phone rang next to Kristin's hospital bed. Before her mom could answer it, Kristin reached over, picked up the phone, and listened for a moment before responding very clearly, "Hi, cousin!"

Without trying, without premeditation or questioning what she could or could not do, she simply grabbed the phone, right on cue. The speech therapist had never witnessed such a dramatic change.

Up to this point, Kristin had focused all her energy on expanding her abilities, one breath, one movement at a time. Now, more aware of herself and her surroundings, her rational mind kicked in—the part of us that can only make meaning by comparison. One of her first fears bubbling up was whether she would be seen as "dumb" by others.

Here was an honor student who couldn't remember events from a few moments ago, struggling to find a word to express a thought. It was heartbreaking to hear her ponder, not her amazing progress, but her deficiencies. She would say, *"Sorry for being so stupid," "I am so slow," "I can't remember..."* She also voiced a flood of misgivings: Would she ever be okay? Would she be able to succeed in school? Would people still like her?

Kristin Challenges Her Own Perspective

My wife Elke, who basically lived at the hospital during this period, sat down with Kristin and gently reminded her of the power of perspective and how her thoughts and words could become self-fulfilling. She pointed out to Kristin how Eron and her mom had talked to her when she couldn't speak, held her hand when she couldn't move, and stayed by her side during uncomfortable medical treatments.

Hadn't she somehow felt their presence, even in a coma? Hadn't her eyes teared up slightly when a family member came in the room? Didn't she understand how much of a sign this had become for us that the Kristin we knew was still here with us?

Elke told Kristin how, days before she could open her eyes or directly acknowledge someone's presence, one random twist and a flopped arm happened to clumsily land on Eron's shoulder in an attempt to hug him. If her family could love her as a motionless, helpless lump on a bed, why did she have to meet some self-imposed standard to be valued or accepted now?

Kristin came to savor the idea that, rather than see herself as stupid, she could just as easily explain to others, "My brain is recovering. Thanks for your patience." Or, "I am not able to find the right words sometimes." She saw that she could choose to focus either on her loss and limits, or on her abilities in the moment, and in this way challenge her limits.

She could also choose to find her own unique way of expressing her life fully, no matter what.

The medical staff and Kristin's extended family fully supported her in exploring these unknowns. I heard one doctor, when pressed, respond to the inevitable question, *"Will she ever be normal?"* by stating simply, *"She will be different."*

This wise doctor had carefully drawn a line where the limits of medicine ended, and Kristin's choices began. By not closing the door to any possibility, his statement was clear: Kristin will be in charge of what "different" means to her.

Chapter 7
Some Just Forget to Die

The perception of wholeness is a freely chosen state.
It is the state of realizing that our level of
well-being is independent of any circumstance.

— Author —

Ironically, when people stop striving to change their outer world, their inner world transforms, sometimes bit by bit, sometimes dramatically. Paradoxically, some find themselves healed of supposedly incurable maladies, long after active medical treatment is terminated.

Some just forget to die.

The information in this chapter is what makes for good newspaper headlines. However, I've intentionally buried these choice maker stories and their implications here in the middle of the book. Why? To keep the drama-hungry part of us from being so drawn to stories of unexpected physical cure that they may somehow distort or overshadow the actual components of the Creation Cycle that underlie such spontaneous healings.

Responding Versus Reacting

Wholeness is a state of being we *choose*, an experience we each can open to in *any* moment. From wholeness, there is nowhere to get to, and no need for change. Assuming this stance allows us to *engage* creatively with, rather than merely *react* to, our circumstances.

In the stories told so far of people transforming the quality of their lives by choice, a fascinating by-product may emerge as well: The person dying recovers; the one in the wheelchair gets up and walks; the one with the irreversible brain injury heals.

How can this be so? Is it mere coincidence, or is something else at work?

The point I want to make in the strongest terms is the fact that the physical changes, or healings, come about as *side effects* of a much deeper change within the person. What seems to allow and promote such transformation is letting go control of the outcome and being fully present to the power of choice. The choice to be whole—able—in each moment vanquishes the need to manipulate the external world for survival's sake.

In the wake of this profound shift, an outer change in a choice maker's physical condition sometimes occurs, sometimes not. What's primary is the transformation itself.

Recall that during the early 1980s, Evy underwent her own deep changes, flowering while she was under a death sentence from ALS. (See her story, Chapter 4.) During this time, in her own words, she looked "like Jell-O in a wheelchair."

Accepting, even embracing her own death, Evy sought to have the best death possible by seeking the experience of love. By turning her attention toward something she desired, she discovered an aliveness already within her. She still had the capacity for passionate interests, for volition and vitality. The process eventually brought her to focus on core desires of exploring the essence of forgiveness and love, at which point her life changed in even more profound ways. She had opened to the wonder and splendor of life fully lived—while still strapped into a wheelchair, dying.

By the time I interviewed her in 1988, she had regained full function of her body. A number of years later, I saw her again on a ferry returning from Victoria, British Columbia. I immediately recognized her curly blond hair, the slight limp from the effects of childhood polio as she walked toward me, and her vibrant smile. But I saw no trace of ALS.

I lost track of Evy in the late 1990s and thought she might have finally succumbed to the disease. But as this book was being edited, I found her again—alive and fully engaged in helping others as a minister and pastoral counselor!

Who's Getting the Message?

Evy worked with the medical community through the 1980s and 1990s, researching and speaking to medical professionals about the potential for deeper healing and growth inherent within crisis. She stopped her attempts to carry the message to the medical community, however. Evy found that the field is so strongly goal-oriented—seeking to cure disease and prolong life—that her deepest, most vital message of inward healing, self-growth, and well-being was missed. Whether mainstream or alternative, medical practitioners twisted her message into a recipe for cures.

Findings from Evy's research with ALS patients at the University of Washington after she had experienced her own deep healing show that longevity appeared to be most closely correlated with a person's attitude and active re-engagement in life. By examining a multitude of psychological factors, she found a significant correlation between psychological state and survival: "The results indicate that psychological status is an important prognostic factor in ALS, independent of length of time since diagnosis, disease severity, and age."[13]

Amazingly, these people told her the ALS had opened them to a new dimension of aliveness unseen prior to the disease. Evy agrees from her own experience: "I still struggle physically. I still have arms that are weak and a brace on my leg. But my quality of life is not linked to my physical body."

It's Okay to Be a Slow Learner

I've already recounted how I had not really grasped or applied this message when my own catastrophic seizure in 1997 ended my career as a rehabilitation counselor and precipitated my personal journey through crisis and disability. As noted, all my support systems flowed from the loss of myself as a productive, able-bodied person.

Instead, I'd accepted my doctor's sentence of lifelong disability and the impossibility of my brain healing in any significant way. By contrast, I believe today that the major brain healing I've experienced during the past decade has likely come about as a consequence of my having seized opportunities to move my life in new directions.

So today, I can add my own testimony to that of other choice makers who are succeeding in recreating their lives by acting directly upon new perceptions and desires. We want readers of this book to know that you don't have to be dying or disabled to renew your own life by stepping directly into whatever ability remains to you and following what inspires you.

To echo Emerson: Move confidently in the direction of your own desires, fulfilling to yourself and benefiting others.

Science Weighs In

For generations it's been held as sacrosanct that adult brains, unlike those of children, can't and don't change, even though for several decades now scientists have shown the brain's ability to change *and* heal, both in animals and humans. Acceptance of this evidence has only slowly taken root in the medical community and begun to have some impact on treatment.

Now, remarkable findings from research into the mind's capacity to heal the physical brain and body are rapidly emerging. In *The Brain That Changes Itself,* by Norman Doidge, MD, compelling research carves new territory regarding how our thoughts can radically change the very structure of our brains—how human thought directly affects healing in the body.

Dr. Doidge tells of a sixty-five-year-old poet and college professor in New York, Pedro Bach-y-Rita, who was paralyzed by a stroke, leaving him unable to speak or walk. After four weeks in a rehabilitation center, Pedro showed no signs of improvement and so was discharged. His son George took him from New York back to Mexico where he was attending medical school.

There, he worked with his father daily to strengthen his abilities, strapping knee pads on him and teaching him to crawl:

> *We played games on the floor, with my rolling marbles, and his having to catch them. Or we'd throw coins on the floor, and he'd have to try and pick them up with his weak right hand. Everything we tried involved turning normal life experiences into exercises. We turned washing pots into an exercise. He'd hold the pot with his good hand and make his weak hand—it had little control and made spastic jerking movements—go round and round, fifteen minutes clockwise, fifteen minutes counterclockwise. The circumference of the pot kept his hand contained. These were steps, each one overlapping with the one before, and little by little he got better. After a while he helped to design the steps. He wanted to get to the point where he could sit down and eat with me and the other medical students.*

Pedro's speech began to improve after several months, and he expressed a desire to resume his writing. Dr. Doidge relates,

> *He would sit in front of a typewriter, his middle finger over the desired key, then drop this whole arm to strike it. When he had mastered that, he would drop just the wrist, and finally the fingers, one at a time. Eventually, he learned to type normally again.*

At the end of the year, his recovery was complete enough for Pedro to return to full-time teaching again at City College in New York. He loved it and worked until he retired at seventy. Then he got another job at San Francisco State College, remarried, and kept working, hiking, and traveling. He was active for seven years after his stroke. On a visit to friends in Bogotá, Colombia, he went climbing high in the mountains. At nine thousand feet, he had a heart attack and died shortly thereafter. He was seventy-two.

It happened that Pedro's other son, Paul, was a physician working in San Francisco, where Pedro's body was brought in for an autopsy by Dr. Mary Jane Aguilar. Dr. Doidge quotes Paul's story:

> *A few days later, Mary Jane called me and said, "Paul, come down. I've got something to show you." When I got to the old Stanford Hospital, there, spread out on the table, were slices of my father's brain on slides.*

He was speechless.

> *I was feeling revulsion, but I could also see Mary Jane's excitement because what the slides showed was that my father had had a huge lesion from a stroke, and that it never healed, even though he recovered all those functions. I freaked out. I got numb. I was thinking, "Look at all this damage he has." And she said, "How can you recover with all this damage?"*

When Paul examined the lesion in the brain stem caused by the stroke seven years before, he couldn't comprehend how his father had recovered so much ability when 97 percent of the nerves had been destroyed.

> *I knew that meant that somehow his brain had totally reorganized itself because of the work he did with George. We didn't know how remarkable his recovery was until*

that moment, because we had no idea of the extent of his
lesion, since there were no brain scans in those days. When
people did recover, we tended to assume that there really
hadn't been much damage in the first place.

His father's remarkable recovery triggered a career change for Dr. Paul Bach-y-Rita. He has since become a pioneer in the field of brain plasticity, studying how the brain physically creates new nerve pathways to compensate for brain damage. He's created numerous sensory substitution devices, such as ones that allow blind people to see, or to regain balance from damaged inner ear function.

Improved Lens for Neuroscience

Led by pioneers such as Paul Bach-y-Rita, today's scientists work from a much more powerful map of the mature brain's ability to heal itself. Ironically, they are finding that the brain's capacity to adapt and change can also create rigidity, what Doidge termed "plastic paradox."

He states,

The plastic paradox is that the same neuroplastic proper-
ties that allow us to change our brains and produce more
flexible behavior can also allow us to produce more rigid
ones…Indeed, it is because we have a neuroplastic brain
that we can develop these rigid behaviors in the first place.

But rigid behaviors can soften and transform, resulting in new ways of being. Doidge observes that choice steers the directions our lives will take:

Neuroplasticity is like pliable snow on a hill. When we
go down the hill on a sled, we can be flexible because we
have the option of taking different paths through the soft
snow each time. But should we choose the same path a

second or third time, tracks will start to develop, and soon we will tend to get stuck in a rut—our route now will be quite rigid as neural circuits, once established, tend to become self-sustaining. Because our neuroplasticity can give rise to both mental flexibility and mental rigidity, we tend to underestimate our own potential for flexibility, which most of us experience only in flashes.[14]

It seems likely that taking a creative stance enhances the brain's natural plasticity to adapt to new circumstances—at any age. In contrast, a disability stance actually leads to reduced function and less ability to adapt to new situations. A person's strong intention tends to lead to new insights and creations, but adherence to a problem-centered focus leads to rigidity, limitation, and increased disability. We become frozen to our past.

The Power of the Observer

The implications of new research spanning numerous scientific disciplines—biology, medicine, physics, and psychology—is changing our perceptions of what human beings are capable of achieving in ways that may shake the very roots of science. Just over a hundred years ago, physicists had figured out how the universe worked and even discouraged aspiring students from pursuing a career in such a dead-end field. Then along came the revolutionary theories of relativity and quantum mechanics.

As new sciences mature, ever-new findings birth even more surprises to confound our present interpretations of reality. In the weird world of the tinier than tiny, an atom's anatomy can be observed as a particle or wave, depending on how we choose to peek at it. How can something be both? Or, is it really even something when we are not looking at it? Scientists are not sure.

The separation of observer and observed appears not to be so separate even in our everyday interactions with the world.

Take one example of a rapidly growing body of empirical research emanating from physics, biology, and psychology. William Tiller, PhD, professor emeritus in material science at Stanford University, has experimentally demonstrated that individuals who are capable of maintaining highly focused attention on a flask of water can robustly change its pH level. By clear intention and focused attention, they can raise or lower the pH at will by a factor of ten. Similarly, using only the power of their focused thoughts, subjects were able to speed up or slow down the growth of cell cultures.[15]

Dr. Tiller, among a rapidly growing number of scientists from around the world, is compiling evidence undermining the scientific method as we currently understand it. Current assumptions that undergird science do not adequately take into account the effects of the experimenter's thoughts on experimental results at the macro level. Indeed, the effect of a person's thoughts can change outcomes as well as experimental controls, even when that person is placed hundreds of miles away from the experiment.

Such remarkable results require new maps of our relationship to the whole. Tiller has broadened the compass of Einstein's theory of relativity by expanding his famous formula to bring the mystery of consciousness into the mix. According to this new formulation,

$$Consciousness = Energy = Matter$$

A stunning conception, isn't it? Whether or not Tiller's interpretations hold up, his impressive data, along with those of numerous other researchers, is sketching the outlines to an entirely new map of the relationship between the brain and consciousness. This growing stack of evidence points ever more directly at the ability of our consciousness to affect the world outside the brain cavity—simply by holding a particular intention or belief.

These findings rest uneasily alongside the basic assumptions science has relied on for the last centuries.

Fortunately, the Creation Cycle is alive and well in science. New findings confound accepted theories incapable of embracing them and, at times, cascade the entire field into crisis and chaos. And like the breakup of any accepted belief, such shake-ups in science engender just as much resistance from the established ideologies of this day and age as they did when Copernicus flung the earth out from the center of the universe, only to ignite a revolution in our perceptions of our relationship to the whole.

The Amazing Placebo

By linking the three domains of consciousness, energy, and matter, a whole new coherence emerges out of an array of heretofore-unexplained phenomena. One such problem plaguing scientists is the apparent power of the placebo to effect change in the physical health of individuals.

Hundreds of studies show the power of the mind to affect the physical. For instance, a group of men in one study was given chemotherapy—or so they believed. Actually, they were treated with an inactive saline solution. Twenty percent of the men lost their hair, as they believed would happen with chemo treatment.

Such strong effects from an inactive treatment seem implausible, but think of times when you felt nervous, like standing in front of a group to give a talk. Readily measurable changes in your blood pressure, pulse, and brain activity occurred. All these, too, arise from simple thought.

Although the exact mechanisms governing or evoking the placebo effect have yet to be discovered by scientists, it's clear in some circumstances that our beliefs can change our biochemistry, positively or negatively.

Even Suggestion Comes into Play

It appears the mere suggestion that an intervention might work can change a person's perception and evoke the placebo effect, bringing real physical changes in its wake. In one study, researchers divided in half a group of hotel cleaning maids. Physical testing showed both groups tended towards obesity and de-conditioning. One group was told how their daily activity on the job actually was healthy exercise and would increase their aerobic capacity, strength, and general health. Nothing was told to the other group.

After one month, measurable positive affects in physical well-being were found only in the group of women who believed that their daily routine was beneficial to them.[16]

The power of belief to effect physical changes has broad implications for medicine. To start with, beliefs can influence outcomes for ill as well as for good, since their effects can also correlate with even more trauma.

Numerous double-blind studies, in which neither researchers nor subjects know who is receiving treatment (an actual drug) and who is receiving a placebo, show that physicians' own attitudes about a drug's effectiveness can influence patient outcomes. Such results are poorer for those doctors who doubt the efficacy of the treatment than for those doctors who enthusiastically believe in the drug's effects.

Inconsistent benefits of certain drugs also seem to depend on the particular doctors administering the medication. These conflicts were so apparent that, starting many decades ago, experiments were set up to sort out why. The *American Journal of Psychiatry* in 1959 published a double blind study seeking answers to this puzzle.

In the study, two doctors administered the same drug: one who was enthusiastic about the drug's powerful abilities to cure, and the other an avowed skeptic. Neither doctor knew whether he or she was actually administrating the real drug or the placebo, and none of the patients was even aware of the experiment, so they all thought they were receiving the real drug.

The results? The drug was significantly more powerful than the placebo for the doctor who believed in it, but for the skeptical doctor's patients, no beneficial drug effects at all were observed.[17]

Somehow, the doctor's own beliefs significantly affect a drug's effects, without the patient even realizing it.

These findings have been repeated in numerous experiments, and do not fit easily within currently accepted scientific beliefs about how our thoughts operate. One intent of this book is to suggest the value of using the tools of awareness and choice that we already possess to peer beyond the edges of accepted beliefs. If we are willing to use these tools, we might examine and come to understand disease and its remedy in a new light.

One Chance in Two Hundred?

It's worth pondering the distinct possibility that many doctors, in an attempt to maintain objectivity, may actually be negatively in-fluencing medical outcomes. After my last open-heart surgery, I developed atrial fibrillation resulting in an erratic heartbeat. During one appointment with my cardiologist, he concluded his dire prognosis by stating I had only a one-in-two-hundred chance of ever reversing the condition.

I asked, "Aren't you curious about that *one?*"

His response? "Absolutely not! It's statistically irrelevant. I feel it's important for you to know the facts."

Given the massive amount of data from placebo studies dem-onstrating the power of thought or even suggestion to influence physical changes in the body, such "facts" may actually become self-fulfilling for those patients who hold the doctor to be the pre-eminent expert or who see the door shut tight against other possibilities.

Indeed, by examining that one "exceptional" patient in two hundred, and seeking out other "exceptional" patients from, say, a million people suffering from the same affliction, we now have a group of five thousand "exceptional" patients to study. The patterns observed in this subgroup may lead us to see something *truly* exceptional, which might just blow apart our current maps guiding medicine—if we are willing to let go to new possibilities.

Wayne Johnston's Story

Most medical practitioners and helping professionals pursue treatment of patients in the expectation it will resolve problems and increase quality of life. But it's clear in the stories so far that something more is involved in achieving a higher quality of life experience than mere manipulation of the physical or the length of survival.

Consider Wayne, a tugboat engineer diagnosed with leukemia, who was told by his doctor to put his affairs in order. He was assigned to an oncologist who identified an experimental drug trial and was able to enroll Wayne in the program. The first sequence of treatment brought about a remission that improved his health enough to allow him to enroll in a certification program to become a teacher. This significant life change was a path he had started on when he was younger. Modern medicine had given him a second chance—following through on a dream was a way to bet on life rather than give up.

When he was student teaching, the cancer returned, and he had to undergo a second round of treatment. The first night back in the hospital, before being moved to isolation because his immune system was compromised and the chemotherapy he was receiving was dangerous to others, he watched as the man in the next bed struggled at death's door. Wayne was acutely aware that his own situation mirrored this man's ordeal. At the end of the chemotherapy regimen, he also ended up in intensive care in a fight for his life.

He won another chance, another remission. But life remained very uncertain. And, living with the likelihood that the reprieve would be short-lived caused him to make peace with death. It was clear to Wayne that he still possessed many treasures and untapped potentials—a stance prompting him to action without knowing where it would all lead.

When I met Wayne several years later, he had begun a new career teaching high school English, earning a wage significantly less than what he'd made in the marine towing industry. He'd lost a twenty-year career. He'd nearly lost his life. He was forced to start over at middle age in a new occupation requiring two years' investment in retraining. The potential for reoccurrence of cancer hung ever-present on the horizon.

One day while climbing with Wayne on the flanks of snowy Mt. Baker, I asked him what impact the leukemia had on his life and wasn't shocked by his powerful answer echoing what so many others had told me over the past two decades. "The leukemia was horrible. I wouldn't wish what I went through on my worst enemy. But don't *ever* take it away from me!"

It's easy to imagine the horror of feeling your body waste away, losing your career, and dragging your family to the edge of emotional and financial ruin. But, "Don't ever take it away from me" suggests either lunatic dedication to suffering and sacrifice or words pointing to a hidden, transformative face of crisis.

Wholeness Is Here Now—Russell Targ

Let me pass on to you the story of Russell Targ, retired senior staff scientist for Lockheed Martin and pioneer developer of the laser. Targ was hospitalized in serious condition. In his book, *The Heart of the Mind: How to Experience God Without Belief,* Targ relates what transpired when he released his fears of what might happen, and let go to experiencing each moment:

> *I was being cared for by three doctors in whom I have great confidence. But as I looked up at these wise men standing at the foot of my bed, it was clear they didn't*

know what to do. With tears in my eyes, I faced the real possibility that I might soon die. As night fell, I remembered the teaching that surrender is not the same as giving up…I pursued the well-known mantra "Let go, let God," and listened with my full attention to the Hayden String Quartets a good friend had brought me.

As I became more and more involved with the music, my fear diminished. As I followed the music, measure by measure, the fear disappeared entirely! The scientist part of me was astonished. I discovered I could increase and decrease my experience of fear by opening and closing the temporal width of my window of attention. Realizing that the present moment is free of fear, I went to sleep and woke the next day on the road to recovery.

The important lesson for me is that both fear and oppression reside in the future, based on impressions from the past. The opportunity to change your mind and find peace, meaning, and love in the midst of strife has been taught for thousands of years. The reason it has fallen into neglect in the scientific age is that the path resides in experience rather than analysis. [18]

Me Again

It's true that we take the simplest things in life for granted, until they slip just beyond reach.

I felt I understood what Russell Targ was talking about. In 1988, a few months after my first son was born, I experienced something akin to what he describes. Money had steadily drained from our bank account as both my wife and I tried to start a new business just as our first child was born. Compounding our problems, my chronic back pain from a bulged disc disabled me from most daily activities for several months. I found myself bedridden for days at a time, suffering from low back spasms.

My life was slowly spiraling out of control. Depression began to overtake my days like an insidious vine choking out the light. I remember in particular one episode of spasms that trapped me in bed for several days when my son Ryan was about six months old. Movement for me had become excruciating and getting out of bed unthinkable, so I couldn't participate in changing his diaper, much less pick him up or play with him.

For hours, sometimes days, I couldn't even get up to go to the bathroom for myself. My dreams of taking my little son fishing and climbing, of showing him the world of adventure, seemed far beyond the reach of reality. Perhaps they were dashed forever. Maybe I would never walk normally again ... each catastrophic thought deepened my depression and hopelessness.

Then I saw the cobweb.

The afternoon sun sparkled off intricately spun spider silk clinging to the corner of the room. Its very presence mocked me. Why, I couldn't even get up to scrape a silly cobweb off the wall!

My emotions followed my thoughts into total dismay. How can I ever successfully accomplish anything when I can't even clean up a wispy cobweb? I felt helpless and hopeless.

In the midst of my pain and depression, a small quiet thought floated through my head. "You know, Jim, that cobweb is large enough and dusty enough that it might even pre-date your injury. You never entertained thoughts of ending your life over a cobweb before."

At the time, I'd already interviewed a number of people dealing with much more severe crises than I faced, but who were living peace-filled, fulfilled lives in spite of their limitations.

Well, I thought, if they can do it, so can I.

Or maybe not. My optimism immediately crashed into a brick wall of reality. I still can't get out of bed to wipe up a cobweb, much less pick up my baby! I can't even get up to pee. I can't ... I can't ...

So it went, back and forth for the next two days. Finally, exhausted and embarrassed about my unwillingness to choose thoughts other than those leading me directly into a black hole of hopelessness, I made a deal with myself: *Jim, take ten minutes out to see the world differently. See what you already do have right now, just as you are. You aren't totally helpless. Focus on what does work in your body and which abilities you do have right now.*

I scolded myself, thinking that I could always go back to my suffering afterwards. For some reason, this deal shot a little shiver of excitement through me. (In retrospect, I think the excitement sprang more from the realization I didn't have to deny my deep suffering and pain, rather than from the prospect of making a true change in my life.)

I thought of my favorite role model for vibrancy in the face of adversity, Evy McDonald, diagnosed with ALS in 1981. My God, if Evy could radically transform her own self-identity while staring death in the face, then *I* can see something besides the limitations of a non-lethal back injury!

Although it seemed a little silly to be playing Pollyanna, I had ten minutes, so I dove into it.

At first, I reverted to something my mind knew to do well. I made comparisons. Robotically, I mouthed the words, *I can see my son; I could be blind too. I can feel my full bladder; I could be incontinent. I can feel the throbbing pain; I could be paralyzed and numb. I can hear the traffic outside; I could be deaf.*

Along came the predictable flood of objections: *But I still can't pick him up … I still can't get up … I still may not ever be able to take my son fishing.* Still, I kept making a conscious choice to see what ability I already possessed.

But I also allowed myself to acknowledge my pain and limitation. This approach was more difficult at first, but it eliminated the need to value only positive thoughts by contrasting them with a negative thought. And so:

I can see my son…
I can feel my body all the way to my toes…
I can feel pain in my back and also feel the tension in my jaw
   and arms…
I am aware how depressed I've been.
The warmth of the room trickled into my awareness.
I have the ability to hear my son's yips of excitement springing
from the carpet below. I have eyes to see him playing happily amidst
the very pile of wooden blocks and train tracks I played with at his
age.

I repeated the words by rote, with nothing but my intention to see more than the pain and limitation I felt, all the while observing my body wracked in pain, my full bladder straining, not resisting the pain but allowing it as another sensation.

A few more minutes passed by.

Suddenly, I became aware of actually being interested and engaged in my son's play. This was new! Just watching a baby at play engaged and pleased me, instead of his mere presence triggering more grief about my inability to play alongside him.

Where did those suddenly warm feelings come from? For weeks I'd known nothing but pain, depression, grayness. Something new had definitely awakened inside me.

I continued. *I can see the clouds outside my bedroom.*

White puffs hanging from a light-blue sky morphed into a dragon. A television set chased by a Volkswagen with a turtle on top floated slowly across the window.

Unexpected feelings of well-being floated above my horizon.

Thoughts of childhood days suddenly bubbled into my consciousness—kids from our neighborhood lying in the summer grass and projecting outrageous silent movies into the clouds above us. These contained all sorts of sinister or comical plots, all transforming themselves into new characters and twisted story lines spurred by a moment's whim.

A few more moments. Minutes. Or, maybe hours? I lost all track of time as a fine vibration engulfed my body, spinning me out of time and space. Bemused, I felt my whole body seemingly expand into the air around me, enveloping me in a womb of indescribable peace and unity. Acceptance and well-being melted the confusion and permeated my every cell.

I felt totally fulfilled. Inexpressible love washed through me.

Everything I ever wanted, everything I ever sought in my life I was finding right there—still in bed, flat on my back. I'd never experienced anything like it before in my whole life.

For hours more I lay, still bedridden and in constant pain, unable to get up to pee or play with my son or clean up a cobweb, but now I found my world awash in peace and joy.

No words can encompass what I experienced. No way was I able to contain or understand the fullness of peace surrounding and filling me; its breadth and depth exploded beyond description. Yet nothing had changed in my world except my willingness to set my intention, and my attention, toward seeing wholeness all around and in me, inclusive of the pain.

My sense of well-being and peace persisted for the next several days, gradually tapering off from the intensity of the first minutes and hours, but still palpably present in my every action and thought.

Here I need to mention one lesser effect of my experience, at least in comparison to the utter peace surrounding me. This was a physical healing. Hour by hour, the back injury site gradually changed. Over the course of the first twelve hours, my back problem entirely resolved. The physical changes, of course, were most welcome; but they could add nothing to my already complete state of peace.

What had precipitated this transformation in awareness and well-being? People who believe in miracles would point to God. Rational scientists, without independent and reproducible studies to consult, wouldn't attempt to pronounce on causation. Did the bulged disc resolve as a result of my actions, or was this result merely coincidental with other factors?

The Paradox of Wholeness

Where science can help, however, is by seeking and documenting patterns of response and outcomes among people who exhibit similar perceptual shifts. Perhaps such shifts entrain physical changes as well. By following the evidence, we might challenge those unquestioned assumptions and perspectives concerning what constitutes true healing that currently guide medical research and practice.

As caregivers in helping institutions, we may also discover more powerful ways to support individuals struggling with life challenges—to help them open to an inner richness and quality of life even as we work to help them change the conditions of their outer world.

Lest we fall back into a perspective of seeking "inner peace" as a new medical treatment, however, we need to stay clear about what the above stories really tell us. Wholeness and well-being do not necessarily lead to physical cure or fixing problems. The Creation Cycle suggests *a way of being*—not a treatment plan.

In this paradox lies much of the confusion over the myriad techniques and treatments extolled by New Age tomes that reckon too simplistically on the role of intention or positive thinking in manipulating physical healing.

Once a person shifts to a creative perspective, he or she naturally assumes a stance of ability—wholeness—a stance transcending circumstance. A side effect of physical healing follows for some, and not others. For all, however, it was the experience of becoming the creative force in their own life that was an end in itself, since this stance is self-chosen and not dependent upon any external factors.

Viktor Frankl observed the same relationship between self-actualization and self-transcendence in his book *Man's Search for Meaning*. He writes:

> *The true meaning of life is to be found in the world rather than within man or his own psyche, as though it were a closed system ... Human experience is essentially self-transcendence rather than self-actualization. Self-actualization is not a possible aim at all, for the simple reason that the more a man would strive for it, the more he would miss it ... In other words, self-actualization cannot be attained if it is made an end in itself, but only as a side effect of self-transcendence.*[19]

Flipping the Switch

Here's an example of the power of self-transcendence from my own recent experience. It happened after I recovered from my second open-heart surgery in 2005 to replace the artificial valve that had been ticking in my chest for thirty years. The surgery was a success since I'm here to write these words, although my heart hasn't figured how to accommodate so much trauma from two surgeries and a mass of artificial patches and a new valve, so it beats erratically and inefficiently.

While driving to work one day a year after the second surgery, my thoughts wandered to an early morning walk with my wife, where she had patiently waited for me to catch up to her after each slight hill. I was forced to stop every few feet to catch my breath and let my heart settle back into a more restrained gallop before moving on. I couldn't ride a bicycle. I couldn't go running with my kids ...

Seeing how limited my life had become once again, a familiar pall of depression seeped into me. Recognizing that I was allowing my circumstances to define my well-being, I refocused my attention. Now, while observing my thoughts and feelings carefully, I also allowed the despondent feelings to sweep through without resistance.

Looking out the car window, I let go to just being in the experience of feeling depressed while driving a fourteen-year-old car with over two hundred thousand miles on it, rattling down a forested road dappled by an early spring sunrise. As I observed my emotions, thoughts, body sensations, and senses, a very different world suddenly revealed itself.

Bright green buds sparkled from last night's rain. My eyes swept from the green-carpeted forest floor to the yellow flash of flowers blossoming atop early-spring skunk cabbage as I flew past at fifty miles an hour. Sunlight and shadow danced across my arms. Musicians impossibly stuffed into my dashboard played Bach's Toccata and Fugue in D Minor, permeating the air around me. A flip of a switch adjusted the temperature in the car—there, just the way I wanted it.

Why, the richest man in the world couldn't experience this even a century ago! What an amazing gift!

My spine tingled as a sense of fullness and joy surged through me. Peace and well-being permeated my every cell. A timeless expansiveness enveloped me, very much like when I was down flat on my back with that injured disc so many years ago.

In that moment I knew without equivocation, without doubt, all that matters is the magnificence of our own presence and the choices we make. Just now.

No, my heart didn't suddenly fix itself. But it did not matter.

Chapter 8
How We Institutionalize Disability

I know I am solid and sound,
To me the converging objects of the universe flow,
All are written to me,
and I must get what the writing means.

— Walt Whitman, "Song of Myself" —

I am in part a product of the miracle wrought by modern medicine's magic. These technological advances have kept me alive
long enough to write these words, so I am not in any way attempting to diminish the medical world's triumphs. I only wish
to help open a window to how institutional medicine can better
support the people it serves.

Today's technologies vanquish, or at least contain, many foes.
For example, smallpox and polio grab little of our attention today when only a couple of generations ago whole nations bowed
to their effects. But even as science masters many diseases by its
ingenuity and expertise, new fears seem to slide into the place of
the defeated enemies.

Especially since the advent of the germ theory, medicine has
increasingly organized itself around a perspective of disease identification and eradication. The incredible success of certain drugs
that have essentially eliminated whole classes of disease, as well
as the advent of sophisticated surgical and other treatments, has
helped millions circumvent the pits of crisis, pulling them out
of the otherwise bottomless abyss of chronic disability or death.

Next Magic Bullet, Please

Thus our medical system has given hope to many where no hope existed. But it has also inadvertently done something else; it has diminished individual responsibility for one's own well-being. Our reliance on medical experts and social services to solve our problems has created a dependency on the very systems ostensibly designed to help us heal and move on.

The incredible advances of medical technology over the last century have effectively narrowed our search for a cure down to discovering the next magic bullet to blast away whatever ails us. This search has become a task for the professionals, not patients.

It's sobering to note how many of the critically or terminally ill people I interviewed over the last twenty years identified their change point as coming *after* the moment the doctors exhausted all treatment options, thereby effectively cutting that last cord of hope for survival. All these choice makers, on their own accord, had become the masters of meaning and purpose, taking the reins of their own creative power with the capacities remaining to them.

Their stories are a testament to the power to make a difference in their own well-being, but our medical system, by its focus on problem elimination and dependency on highly trained experts, effectively discourages such possibilities.

Can We Switch Out of Autopilot?

That's not to say that choice makers act independently from the expert care of their doctors—far from it. But by examining the stories of people traversing crisis to realize higher qualities in life, we can see how each discovered something essential: The journey has to be self-piloted. No family member, loved one, doctor, insurance company, or government department can choose our own individual path of discovery and transformation for us.

We go to the doctor because we have a problem. "Doc, it hurts here." "This doesn't work anymore." "It's broken. Can you fix it?" "My stomach sends food back up and not down where it's supposed to go." "My brain feels like a sieve letting my thoughts leak out." "Help me ..."

So we pay an expert to fix the problem. If the problem careens us off the beaten track into unknown territory, and if no answers readily present themselves, we tend to look increasingly to the experts for solutions.

Helping institutions would be much more effective if the insights of the Creation Cycle were fully incorporated into a more integrated approach to rehabilitation. Such a recovery model would embrace both the expertise of our current systems and the power of each individual to shift focus away from battling problems toward becoming responsible for creating anew.

Breaking Out of the Mold

Ken labored for years with diabetes, a damaged heart, arthritis, and Parkinson's disease. His right arm had been deformed and rendered almost useless in a motorcycle accident as a teenager. However, he more than compensated for his disabilities and worked successfully as a custodian for thirty-eight years, until he twisted his good arm out of its shoulder joint while torquing a rust-encrusted valve.

Before the last accident, his intention obviously followed a creative, ability-centered stance. When confronted by a task needing two strong arms or good aerobic capacity, he successfully found ways to get the work done in spite of his limitations. Over the years, as new challenges arose, Ken masterfully adapted, like a ship adjusting its sails to stay on course in contrary winds.

But now he'd injured his remaining good arm, rendering him *fully disabled.* What stance would he take? One of disability or ability?

Let's follow Ken as he wends his way through the medical and rehabilitation system. First, he confronts the usual flood of forms to fill out. Next, he labors through a routine gauntlet of exams, X-rays, MRIs, and blood tests. Finally, he sits in on the exam table waiting to hear what's in store for him.

It's bad news. The doctor explains to Ken that he's torn his rotator cuff—a spur on the bone and old scar tissue will need surgery to heal properly. Months pass as Ken waits for authorization from his insurance company to have the surgery. Unable to take action on his own behalf, he now must depend on others to fix his problem. He waits … and waits …

Finally, his workers' compensation adjudicator authorizes the new surgery, and Ken undergoes the procedure. Recovering from the surgery, he again goes into wait mode until its effects can be assessed, like a ship stranded until fresh winds stir it to life. He waits more than a year to hear the official determination: His surgery has failed to cure the problem. Despite the good efforts of his doctors and rehabilitation specialists, he now has only partially restored function to his shoulder.

Meanwhile, Ken has slowly become the passive observer of his own drama. He finds himself surrounded by experts who are busy identifying his problems, as well as which of the available resources might defeat or at least control them. He undergoes a second surgery, which stops some of the pain but in the end leaves his arm scarred and even more limited.

By the time I met with him, Ken had come to perceive his world from a very different perspective. He showed me his arms, one crippled by the motorcycle and the other left useless by the two surgeries. I also heard about the Parkinson's, diabetes, arthritis, newly discovered high blood pressure, and a string of other problems.

The rehabilitation system had never lost sight of the solution to what it considered the priority issue, which was Ken's non-functional shoulder. His employer, insurance adjudicator, doctor, therapist, and counselors all adhered to a common recovery goal:

Fix his shoulder, and if it's not repaired properly, compromise by finding lighter-duty work he could perform.

Here in my office, Ken could not see any possibility of working in any capacity given his myriad disabilities. True, the rehabilitation system might retrain him for an entry-level office job, which the doctors tell him he could perform. He might also use voice-activated software to eliminate having to use his hands. An ergonomic chair could help, and other aids might make it feasible for him to return to work.

But even with all this help, he would have to begin afresh in an unfamiliar, entry-level job, starting over at a fraction of his old salary. Most people in his situation hunker down to defend their disability and fight for a pension. With their livelihood destroyed, it seems few options remain.

Over the following months, as I worked to support him through the protracted medical process, I watched Ken retreat from his former can-do stance to one of seeing only his problems. When I reflected this back to him, he immediately saw what he'd done—he was headed, he told me, toward what he called the "CBC"—Cry Baby Club.

Ken clearly wanted to get the most out of his life. When confronted with the choice between starting over with the meager resources provided through his insurance or taking charge of his own life to explore something new, he didn't hesitate: "I'm not about to start over at sixty years old!"

He proceeded to talk over his limited options with his wife at home. Then, together, they laid out a plan of action focused on Ken's usual can-do attitude, one that built on what they already had. At his next appointment, he came in recharged with enthusiasm.

"We decided to sell the house and use the money to buy a motor home. We'll travel with the years we have left to us. Once my medical treatment is completed, and the docs get as much motion in the shoulder as possible, I'm closing my claim and retiring. I expect to start my new life in about three months."

Ken consciously chose to let his old life die and focus on how to create something new and enriching with what remained to him. Unfortunately, his case is the bold exception.

Social workers, doctors, and rehabilitation professionals all see self-esteem and inner motivation slip downstream when their patients cannot envision a way to return to functional life, thus drifting slowly into a stance of disability.

"It's Up to You Guys Now!"—Thomas's Story

That's what happened to Thomas, a supervisor and business manager ten years younger than Ken, who was well-educated and not challenged by nearly so many problems. But, unlike Ken, he never turned the corner to take command of his power to choose again.

I remember watching him as he sat on the exam table in his doctor's office. It was a critical moment. His doctor had just told him that no surgery would relieve his back pain. Thomas looked defiantly at both of us: "Well, I've done everything I can. It's up to you guys now!"

Here was a man who had just abdicated his life to the professionals attempting to aid him. And the penalty for surrendering all his options? Monthly living expenses paid by his disability insurance, mandated by the workers' compensation system to continue to pay benefits until he could function on his own again.

So why bother risking failure by attempting to meet a new challenge? What hidden dangers lay waiting down that road winding into an uncertain future? Staying disabled morphs into the safest option, albeit a compromising and sad pathway to the future.

A Mixed Agenda—Dan's Story

Becoming chronically disabled and dependent on medical and social systems can be a way to hide other agendas, such as neuroses, self-esteem issues, and fears. For Dan, it might have been a combination. After getting fired from his job, Dan filed complaints with six state and federal watchdog agencies, accusing his company of safety and pollution violations. He also filed several claims for injuries on the job, including injuries to his back and hand, three of which were accepted.

By the time he was referred to me for assistance getting back to work, it was clear Dan found himself sandwiched between vengeance and wanting to get on with life. He never tired of talking about how he stuck it to his company by filing all those complaints, but he didn't seem to see the trap he'd laid for himself.

Not seeing the connection between his injury and his vendetta, he grew visibly impatient about not recovering so he could get back to a productive life again. But how could he possibly get better? That would be acquiescing, admitting defeat in this attack against his boss.

And yet, Dan was clearly bored. His benefits really didn't cover much more than basic bills and food on the table. He certainly wasn't highflying in Vacationland.

Despite doing little on his own behalf, however, he put on quite a show. Once I reached out to him to shake hands when he limped through the office door. Jerking back dramatically and holding his hand safely out of reach, he cried, "Don't you remember? The doctor told me not to use my hand!" My attempt to elicit his signature on a medical release met the same fate.

It's worth noting that when I reviewed Dan's file, I discovered a dozen lengthy, handwritten letters addressed to the authorities meticulously describing his employer's transgressions. And, of course, he somehow found a way to dress himself and drive to our appointments.

People like Dan burden medical and social services, escalating its costs and dampening its potential to achieve successful outcomes. However, the disability focus of the "helping systems" actually encourages abdication of personal responsibility, increasing dependency and setting costs spiraling. By focusing only on fixing the problem in order to return to the precrisis state, much is lost, both by the system that pays for ineffective treatment and by the patients who remain unaware of other options for personal renewal.

In this way, the Creation Cycle is short-circuited: The person undergoing "rehabilitation" need never confront and move through fear or step into unknown territory. Take Terry, for instance.

Who's in Charge Here Anyway?—Terry's Story

After sustaining a debilitating back injury working as a logger, Terry received funds to attend a trade school to gain the skills needed for a less physical job. He now planned to become a medical technician. Highly motivated, Terry actively refocused his full efforts into his new career path. Midway through his first semester, however, his wife was seriously injured in an auto accident.

Juggling classes, homework, and being by his wife's side in the hospital, Terry had to cooperate closely with his teachers to keep up with his coursework, even as he missed numerous days of class. It worked, all except for math class. Even before his wife's accident, he'd struggled to learn some new math skills and barely squeaked through the exams during his first semester.

After taking the summer off to rest, a very different Terry sat down in my office. He was starting the fall semester with a whole array of pains and problems that now seemed to block him from even getting into classes. "I'm not sure I can walk across campus." "I sprained my ankle this summer." "I'm not sure my doctor will let me go since my heart trouble flared up too."

I assured him that we could get a disability permit for parking, get crutches or a cane by a doctor's prescription, a wheeled book bag, even a wheelchair if necessary. He parried each suggestion, coming up with new problems as fast as the old ones were solved. Finally, he pulled the trump card. "I'll wait until the doctor tells me what I can do. I can't go to school without his permission."

After his next appointment showed no change toward a positive stance, I decided to call Terry's doctor, who explained: "Terry told me his pain levels are through the roof. He can't sleep. He cannot concentrate or even take care of his basic needs. I don't see how he could go to school so I'm pulling him out."

So who was in charge here?

It's striking that Terry's stance of disability was diametrically opposite to how he acted during his wife's recovery only a few months before. Clearly, something else was going on. But the real issue remained hidden, unacknowledged, and unsolved while his growing lists of problems strained the safety net afforded by the disability system.

At our next appointment, instead of confronting him head-on about his sudden change of stance, I asked him about his long-term goals and interests. Off-handedly, during one response, he commented, "I'm interested in sales, and I don't really see a need to take the math for that type of job."

Seeing an opening, I agreed. "We could easily modify your schedule to include one more marketing class and eliminate the math class."

The old Terry suddenly resurfaced, motivated and directed. Amazingly, it turned out that his entire college career had stumbled over the fear of failing one class. (Sound familiar, anyone?) But unless he saw the pattern and confronted it, the next failed class or another unresolved fear would send him spiraling right back into a disability stance.

Disability may be miserable. But it's safe.

Helpers Can Only Do So Much

Before crisis intruded, life was okay. Real enough, anyway. We knew our place. We knew our worth and purpose, which roles to play. This is the precrisis state, the one we reflexively fight to get back to when disaster strikes. When our "normal" is threatened, never mind the tedious job, nagging Aunt Matilda, whining kids, or those constant bills sapping the bank account. It's what we know.

Our life might not add up to much, but it sure beats free-falling into the unknown. We'd rather scramble madly into the arms of the devil we know and the security of the "good old days."

The same dynamics underlie our present medical system, which is driven by the twin goals of fixing problems and defending against future threats. The last two components of the Creation Cycle—chaos and new creation—don't ever come into play on any sustained basis.

In fact, until recently our medical and psychological systems perceived human health in much the same way as we view a brand-new car. This year's shiny new model rolling off the assembly line can be seen as the precrisis state, 100 percent normal. We carefully and proudly drive the thing home, wash and wax and care for it. But it's never quite the same again. Wear and tear inevitably set in. Little pockmarks in the paint and on the windshield, the kid's bubble gum on the seat, coffee decorating the upholstery, that little rattle inside the dash. Then that drunk driver behind you who forgot what his brakes were for crunches your bumper.

The problem and the solution are obvious. We have a clear picture of what the car should look like. We pay the experts to pull out the dents, replace parts, and paint it to its precrisis shiny newness. Or we just replace the darn thing with the latest shiny new car.

Hmm, humans and cars—two different creatures! No amount of outside assistance can uncrunch us after a head-on collision with crisis. Our rearview mirror shows us a better past, one we can't reclaim. Unless we are supported in finding the guideposts to a new life direction, we may idle permanently at the crossroads.

Those of us in the helping professions who are aware of a creation track available to clients and who are willing to support them in moving toward it may well offer the last, best hope for emergency roadside assistance.

Oftentimes in the past, doctors would bombard me with requests to please somehow counter the medically irresolvable handicaps and suffering the patient was experiencing. "Jim, can't you get her a new job?" "This man needs a new career. His back will never be the same." "Can't you at least send her to school?" "If I release him, you'll make sure he gets back to work, won't you?"

The failure of physicians to eliminate their patients' suffering and pain prompts them to seek other ways and means to help the person hobble back into life. Not that all possible ways and means shouldn't be made available, but unless the individual in question actively engages a creative stance, no array of resources will successfully counter identification with the past. Patients will remain in its thrall as they continue to see themselves as disabled and un-abled.

At the Edge Where Help Stops—Randy's Story

Randy, a former construction foreman, provides a good example of how we negate our creative capacity when the limits of the helping systems are not clear. After completing extensive rehabilitation programs, including a comprehensive pain clinic, he knew he might never walk again on his shattered leg, a brutal reminder of the unseen drunk driver who careened from the mists of a dying day.

With assistance from pain management specialists, rehabilitation counselors, physical therapists, and psychologists, Randy set out to create a new life. Using his management skills, he found financial backing to start his own business. But at the point he was ready to close his claim, the disability perspective roared back. "I can't afford to close my claim. I'd lose my disability check every month!"

Suddenly, problems cropped up, and as each one was resolved by his doctor, therapist, or counselor, new issues mysteriously surfaced. In one moment, Randy enthusiastically took the reins of his own life, happily engaging himself in new ways. Then, as if a switch had been flipped, I saw a man, angry, depressed, limited, and trapped.

"You guys will hear from my attorney! I've suffered for five long years. I'll be in pain for the rest of my life! If they only give me a twenty-thousand-dollar settlement, they're in big trouble. No one has ever suffered more than I have!"

I asked Randy how much money would compensate him for the pain and years lost.

Silence.

Finally, he stumbled, "I don't really know." Ultimately, whatever the figure, it could never be enough.

I noted that when Randy flipped into his disability stance, he couldn't see the difference between creative and problem-centered perspectives. His mind riveted itself only on the suffering and loss brought on by that drunk driver five long years ago.

Fighting Disability Creates Disabled People

I was part of and now personally benefit from a rehabilitation system that pours millions of dollars into colleges and trade schools to retrain injured workers. Did you know that no official statistics are kept on the success of such retraining? This is perhaps for good reason.

Professionals who oversee the schooling of men and women with disabilities estimate successful outcomes to occur in only

10 to 20 percent of cases, unless the student is advancing a career already established before becoming disabled.

For example, a carpenter retrained as a construction manager has a good chance of succeeding, since retraining is seen as career advancement and not having to start over. Many people do complete their training in new careers, but with no real change in perspective from their life before crisis, they see little option but to return to their old job and tough it out. It's the life they've always known—it's reality. Their old lifestyle before the injury was built around their wage and job status. Starting over in a new job means diminished status, lower pay, and no guarantee of success.

The ones who do succeed are easy to spot. They exhibit the very patterns of creative renewal seen in the choice maker's response to crisis—regardless of severity of injury, financial distress, level of family support, job skills, or education level.

What drags down the best efforts of well-trained, dedicated medical and helping professionals is the disability perspective itself, which focuses on the crisis phase. The rehabilitation process, particularly the insurance-driven systems, traps itself within its own mission of fighting disability. By effectively riveting attention on the perceived barriers to healing and identifying these as the "real problem," our current helping systems divert all resources to reacting to the problem rather than pointing the way to creative renewal and fulfillment.

Predictably, the people undergoing rehabilitation will retreat into a disability stance within a few months after an unresolved crisis. If they remain on disability for more than a couple of years, they have an extremely high risk of becoming permanently molded to that stance. Only deep inner discomfort will impel them toward their own individual change point … to step off the edge into the unknown.

Chapter 9
Empowered Helping Systems

When it came to my rehabilitation,
I was ultimately the one in control
of the success or failure of those caring for me.

— Stroke survivor Jill Bolte Taylor —

Our medical system and social services handle the first rehabilitation track—helping people cope with immediate medical issues and new disabilities—exceptionally well. Ideally, a more open-ended second track, characterized in these pages as a "creation track," would also come into play. Based on the ready wisdom of the Creation Cycle, such a track would operate in tandem with current interventions, encompassing all aspects of a disabled person's recovery and well-being.

Together these two tracks would provide a continuum of optimal care for treating the presenting problems while simultaneously opening the opportunity for growth.

Role Reversal Is Key

To be truly effective, adding a second track would require a fundamental reversal of roles within our helping systems. The recovering person would be in charge of his or her choices, and the institution or helper would respond accordingly to employ appropriate support and resources. The inherent limitations in any helping system can be effectively employed by using the institutional limitations as the departure point for the person to assume responsibility for further creation and growth.

In short, effective helping systems seek to fix what's broken to mitigate people's pain and suffering while still honoring the power of crisis as a change and growth agent, so that patients themselves are allowed to be in charge of their own creative capacities.

Consider the powerful testimony of former patient Jill Bolte Taylor, a neuroanatomist and national spokesperson for the Harvard Brain Tissue Resource Center. Dr. Taylor recounts the harrowing story of her own ten-year-long rehabilitation from a massive stroke in the left hemisphere of her brain in her memoir, *My Stroke of Insight: A Brain Scientist's Personal Journey.* In a striking passage, she describes her response to an encounter with a busy medical student shortly after being hospitalized. Unfortunately, the young woman was in a hurry and yelled at her as if she were deaf, not a stroke patient. Deeply put off, Dr. Taylor chose to not respond to the treatment, no matter how beneficial it might have been for her. By observing her own response to how the medical student and other staff acted toward her, she realized the impact of her own choices on treatment outcomes. In her words:

> *The biggest lesson I learned that morning was that when it came to my rehabilitation, I was ultimately the one in control of the success or failure of those caring for me. It was my decision to show up or not.*[20]

Dr. Taylor calls attention to a provocative and hidden issue: How can institutions and helping professionals nurture a patient's full participation in their own recovery? This surely is an essential component of any creative recovery program. According to Dr. Taylor, a hospital's first responsibility should be to protect patients' energy levels. *"I responded positively to positive treatment."*

From her own working premise that she was ultimately the one in charge of the success or failure of those caring for her, Dr. Taylor gradually engaged the Creation Cycle, over time radically recreating her life—and life view.

Systems Shift?

Paul Brenner, MD, in his article, "The Five Stages of the Healer," comments on the difference between how our current medical models and exceptional patients (such as Dr. Taylor) perceive their illnesses. He asks,

> *Can we look at illness through another perspective? Is there the possibility that the healing arts in the future will honor that illness can be a friend, and within that dark shell of loneliness that is found within illness is the pearl of the creative, transformational process?*

Dr. Brenner found some cancer patients drastically changed their priorities as a direct result of their illness. He observed that everyday experiences become dramatically more vivid after the diagnosis and concludes:

> *If the healer could assist the ill in finding the deeper meaning to life, then illness itself could be transcended to a new awareness and so to a renewed zest for life. In this stage the healer shifts his focus to the quality of life rather than to the sole importance of the quantum of life.*[21]

A broken bone is painful and involves emergency medical attention and rehabilitation, and the desired result is no more than a return to precrisis normalcy. However, when a person's life is irrevocably changed via crisis, she or he needs to know that the pathways to growth and transformation lie through the problem itself.

The Patient Takes Charge

Once patients are truly supported in moving past the crisis posed by their medical issues, they can engage in the full Creation Cycle. Like Dr. Taylor, they can open to what's fresh and life-giving in their experience, including their caregiving environment. This way, they are also in the best possible position to use the benefits bestowed by the extraordinary expertise of today's medicine.

Remember, in a best-case rehabilitation scenario, both crisis and creation work side-by-side, but the relationship between patients and practitioners changes radically. Patients become the leaders, commanding what choices will be honored. The practitioner's job is to honor those choices. Others may help provide resources or insight, but only the patients can choose to engage themselves within a context of ability.

Having been told he could be retrained for an entry-level job and seeing his disability claim closed, Ken, the custodian who lost the use of both of his arms, at first fought back fiercely. But when shown that his perspective still focused on the loss and victimization he felt, he began to work with his counselor to explore other choices open to him. By taking charge of his own life direction again, Ken underwent a radical shift. He suddenly could see the possibility of other options available to him, such as updating training in his field or taking an early retirement and traveling in an RV with his wife. In this way, he was able to connect with wholly different ways of taking action in his own behalf—and he did.

Since Ken's life had already featured many episodes of successfully challenging adversity, he readily climbed back into the driver's seat.

By contrast, Terry was not so practiced as Ken at overcoming adversity. Here was a young man who'd nearly completed retraining before dragging himself back into a disability stance. As we saw earlier, his goal vanished as unachievable because he couldn't deal successfully with his math class. Rather than constructively confront the real issue, Terry was inclined to use his disability as a defense.

Again, however, rather than acquiesce, his counselors kept empowering him to succeed by continuing to see him as able and to search for barriers that might be stopping him short. Once Terry could see the underlying problem—that his fear of math was defeating his dreams—the tension resolved itself, and again Terry's passion to move forward was reasserted. He showed up for his own life.

Helping the Patient Take Charge

With patients turned into choice makers taking full responsibility of their own lives, institutions and helping professionals can follow the person's lead with whatever resources are appropriate and available. Ideally, caregivers embrace strategies encouraging post-traumatic growth (PTG). They can help prompt clients take a creative stance by setting effective limits on the scope of their services and influence. In so doing, they help both themselves and their clients or patients to find that edge where systems support stops and open-ended creation—led by the individual acting on their own unique desires—begins.

Caregivers are often highly empathetic people who may find it difficult to let others in distress take charge of their own recovery. This is exactly the line between care*giving* (empowering others) and care*taking* (doing for them what they could beneficially be doing for themselves).

The possibility for creating anew, just as we are, doesn't equate to "positive thinking," however. Dale Carnegie notwithstanding, the danger in positive thinking lies in the tendency to deny or misinterpret what's really happening. To be whole is also to acknowledge what is so *this moment*, accepting pain, loss, death. And life just now, just today. We have the capacity to embrace it all while knowing we're more than the limits imposed by our circumstances. *Once we let go to embrace our wholeness and ability, the process unfolds naturally.*

Kübler-Ross on Kübler-Ross

A striking example of the journey through trauma and loss can be seen in the last years of Dr. Elisabeth Kübler-Ross, who worked extensively with dying patients and wrote *On Death and Dying,* the groundbreaking book that gave us the "five stages of dying." A series of strokes left her paralyzed on one side, and from the wreckage left behind, she found herself facing the same choices as her patients had had to confront: How to re-engage living?

She reacted to the dismal prospect of incapacitation and paralysis by becoming angry at everything and everyone around her. She felt she could accept death, but could not cope with being in a paralyzed body diabolically trapping an active, undamaged mind.

As a doctor, Kübler-Ross had taught her patients to give themselves permission to vent their anger and rage, as these are natural expressions of her famous stages of dying: denial, anger, bargaining, depression, and finally, letting go to acceptance. As a patient, she discovered others were less willing to watch her own rocky traverse through the stages of loss and dying.

Her anger at being trapped inside a paralyzed body turned off many former admirers. The press chided her for not having a "good" death. Her behavior drove away most of her friends. She lamented, "It's as if they loved my stages but didn't like me being in one of them." [22]

Once she stabilized after her stroke and saw how her ordeal had opened her to a new understanding of unresolved crisis, she teamed with David Kessler, another end-of-life specialist, to co-write *Life Lessons: Two Experts on Death and Dying Teach Us About the Mysteries of Life and Living.*

Her realizations along the way closely reflect the attitudes expressed by conscious choice makers who exhibit a quality of life far exceeding mere acceptance of their limitations—once they let go of their attachment to their precrisis state. Her path through paralysis led to new revelations about the source of happiness:

Happiness comes from seeing ourselves as being okay, just as we are, today, without comparison to others... [23]

Our happiness is determined by how we interpret, perceive, and integrate what happens into our state of mind. [24]

Nine years later, Kübler-Ross revealed a much expanded view of life and death, as reflected in the foreword to her final book, *On Grief and Grieving: Finding the Meaning of Grief Through the Five Stages of Loss.* Lying in her bed surrounded by flowers, she told her coauthor David Kessler,

I know death is close... I now know that the purpose of my life is more than these stages... it is not just about the life lost, but the life lived. [25]

Sound familiar to others transforming their life experience through loss?

Just before her death, in one of her last sessions with David, she reflected how she had come to see her stroke and disability as secreting gifts of growth for her to discover on the journey of life and death. One of the major gifts concerned something she had resisted during a long career of otherwise astounding achievements:

The last nine years have taught me patience, and the weaker and more bed-bound I become, the more I'm learning about receiving love. [26]

Toward Institutionalizing PTG

The five stages of dying identified by Kübler-Ross have been widely adopted by medical professionals to help people through grief of all kinds. One important distinction must be made, however, and that is the original stages were observed in people who were *dying.* The five stages of dying span the first two elements of the Creation Cycle: Crisis and Chaos. Once those dying accept their fate, they are finally ready to let go to more fully embrace the unknown awaiting them on the other side of death's door.

But when a grieving person works through the stages to final acceptance, what then?

The devastation wreaked by crisis can leave the person crippled emotionally, physically, economically, but still alive. His or her journey is not over, but just beginning. How to proceed? An uncertain and unfamiliar future awaits. This journey requires new perspectives and new tools to forge a path into the unknown of a life postcrisis.

Helpers can empower and support the person to become the center of his or her own creations. This can only be accomplished by handing over the reins of responsibility. Only each individual can make the choices and take the actions to carve a new path toward higher levels of life expression, armed with just what remains to him or her.

I hold out a vision: Our helping institutions, without having to change their present disability track, discover the wisdom and cost-effectiveness of adding a creative dimension to their mission. This new dimension places the patient in charge of charting his or her own course to the future, with potential outcomes seen as unlimited. Helping institutions that offer a true renewal track create an atmosphere for people to respond at their highest level, regardless of their circumstance.

Helpers and institutions introduce the possibility and process for achieving growth and transformation throughout the Creation Cycle stages. These two essential elements interweave and flow from one Cycle stage to the next. Through helpers' words and actions, the Cycle is powerfully modeled to the person in need.

Always, the final responsibility for creating anew remains solely within the individual's purview. Consider the case of Warren, a pipe fitter who adamantly demanded surgery to fix his pain after a back injury—and didn't get it.

Warren's Story

When the doctors unanimously agreed that performing the back surgery he wanted would only make his condition worse, Warren slumped into the posture of an old man within a matter of months. Fixated on a cure, he deflected all other medical and rehabilitation assistance. Once it was clear all efforts to eliminate pain and regain his previous function were exhausted, he was referred to what is seen as a last resort when all curative treatment fails: a pain management program practicing the Creation Cycle. There he was challenged by a new perspective. Instead of being offered new hope for a cure or treatment, he was coached on how to mobilize abilities he already possessed.

Over the course of time, Warren began sitting up straight, talking about returning to work, and taking steps to start his own business. The seed of his change in attitude? A foundational acceptance of what was so. Warren later exclaimed: "The first day they sat us down and stated, 'We aren't going to fix your pain. The pain you have today may be the pain you have the day you die. It's time to get on with living.'"

Instead of stooping under life's burden, Warren learned to adjust his car mirror a bit higher so he had to sit up straight to see. Rather than focus on his loss, he was encouraged to transfer his skills as a pipe fitter into working as a safety officer for the plant where he'd been injured.

Pain That Empowers

The pain clinic process echoes many effective recovery programs flourishing today—AA groups, reality therapies, and ability-driven return-to-work programs, to name just a few—that help individuals engage the power of crisis to grow and transform. Their ability-based processes can be best used when introduced as early as possible, concurrently with medical and other treatments.

When systems employ a creation track, it can speed reso-
lution as well as reduce costs. Indeed, by clearly defining their
scope of services, institutions and helpers effectively hand off responsibility for creative recovery to each one of us. Without such
boundaries established, they instead contribute to stagnation in
the crisis phase, whereby a patient may cling to hopes for an institutional "cure" that will never be forthcoming.

In sum, helpers can be very effective in catalyzing PTG by
coaching the patient in the possibility and process for growth.
Caregivers and institutions can more effectively support patients
by addressing all present problems *and* holding open opportunities for them to uncover their own hidden potentials. Following a
dual track—fixing problems *and* encouraging new directions—
keeps costs in check while enhancing outcomes. (For more information, please refer to the tool kit, "How Systems Can Set Up
PTG" at the end of this chapter.)

Needed—A Better Way To Rehabilitate Veterans

Recent scandals helped focus the nation's attention on the inad-
equate care afforded to injured war veterans returning from Iraq
and Afghanistan. Too many lack the preparation they need to
re-establish themselves in a much-changed world.

One veteran at Walter Reed Army Medical Center, who had
incurred a head injury and lost some use of his right arm, found
himself stagnating in the rehabilitation center without the direction or tools to re-enter civilian life. As a young man, he had run
away from school and a violent father, working his own way out
of a community consumed by poverty. He joined the National
Guard and landed a job as a lubrication tech in an auto dealer-
ship. And then he was shipped out to Iraq for two tours of duty,
the second cut short by his injury.

Initial medical care quickly stabilized his wounds. Once these
healed, however, he was summarily discharged without a new

foundation for making his way in life. Unable to return to his job, without dependable family support, and backed by meager education and now useless work experience, his prospects were bleak. No follow-up assistance and training were ever provided.

Duty complete.

But now what? Like too many without support or resources, this vet came to see himself as mutilated and incapacitated. *Disabled.* He began to lose sight of the fact that he'd once overcome great odds to find his way out of grinding poverty. What would become of him?

There are thousands of anonymous veterans like him deteriorating in rehabilitation systems and facing an equally grim life riveted on losses, not options. For any wounded veteran to continue battling adversity without sight of new creative possibilities serves little purpose for themselves or others.

Inner and Outer Empowered Support

Sergeant Bryan Anderson arrived in Iraq strong and healthy but returned to the United States a triple amputee. He too received the medical care he needed for his injuries, but once stabilized, he traveled a very different road than many vets.

We read stories like Bryan Anderson's in magazines and newspapers and think of them as happening to exceptional people who evince a singular will or power or luck that eludes most of the rest of us. Perhaps we conclude that they are special but we are not.

Bryan's story, however, can inspire us to dig a bit deeper for those qualities we already possess. And his story also helps us to see better how we can support and be supported in ways that keep us focused on a creative path. Bryan received empowered support from fellow vets who helped him see beyond the loss.

There's this other triple amputee that I met here who was hit October 27, but a year before me. He helped me through my hardest times. There's four triple amputees.

He was the third and I was the fourth. He's just like me.
He has a little bit longer limbs than I do, and instead of
him missing his left hand, he's missing his right hand.

But to effectively support ability, one must weather the storms of
emotions that can be triggered by a mere look. Support does not
deny the problem but embraces it while peering past its edges.

One day I was in the shower looking at myself, and I kind
of lost it a little bit. That's when my self-consciousness re-
ally shot up. Dude, nobody wants me like this. It went
bad from there. I couldn't sleep. My chest was getting
tight, like I was going to have a panic attack. I didn't
think I was thinking about it. I just started freaking. I
didn't want to be inside. I didn't want to be outside. I
didn't want to be anywhere. I did not want to kill myself,
but I just felt like I didn't want to be anywhere. I didn't
want anybody to be around me.

I tried to get away from here, just so I could clear my
head. Me and my mom spent three days in Vegas. Craps
and blackjack, that's what I like to play.

While they were in Las Vegas, they talked about what kinds of
T-shirt slogans he could make for himself. His mom exclaimed,
"Seventy-five percent off! You should get a shirt showing off your
personality."

Other family members strode right into the fray of supporting the re-creation of Sgt. Bryan. Looking through the huge array
of prosthetic arms and attachments for swimming, tennis, and
playing pool, his grandfather would ask Bryan, "Why aren't you
wearing the hook? It's so much cooler."

Through the dips and valleys of depression and defeat, Bryan
maintained a remarkable balance of ability-centered focus by fully acknowledging his loss and the challenges it presented.

This is the gripper. It's like a robot hand, a stronger tool. There's a sensor on the inner and outer parts of my forearm. All I do is pretend my hand is still there and open and close it. If I want it to close, I make the close-muscle gradually. If I want it to spin inward, I make that close-muscle really fast. This is my baseball mitt, like a lacrosse racket. This is the hook. You can angle it in and out, put a spoon in there or whatever, pick up little stuff with it.

When challenged he acknowledged the difficulties and realities of his loss while maintaining focus on solutions:

When I don't have help, it'll take me ten minutes to put my legs on. The first time I ever did it, it took me an hour. I'm not really going to wear pants anymore unless it's a nice function. It's hard to pull pants over your legs because your feet are straight, and my legs aren't ever going to get cold. And if people see I'm walking with prosthetic legs, they're more likely to get out of my way than accidentally bump into me and knock me down.

I think I have the record for falling in physical therapy, because I try to push myself to the max on these things, and if you're not falling, you're not trying. That's my motto. I don't fall as much anymore, but for a while I pretty much fell a couple times a day… We did a 110-mile bike ride from Gettysburg to Washington, D.C. Sixty miles the first day, fifty miles the second day. Hand cycle, three wheels. I ended up ripping the glove, breaking the hand, breaking the whole socket. I might do it a little differently, but I'm still going to do it. I didn't actually get up water-skiing. I was up for a second, then my arm ripped off and I fell.

Like other choice makers, Bryan could readily sum up his approach to life:

You have two options once this happens: Roll over and die or move on. I chose to move on. I'm still me. I'm just 75 percent off... From every decision you make, you learn something, whether it was the right decision or the wrong decision.

I don't regret anything.[27]

Other soldiers with Bryan at Walter Reed's Mologne House fared less well. A gunner with the Tennessee National Guard, Sergeant David Thomas, lost a leg and suffered traumatic brain injury when he was wounded in Samarra, just north of Bagdad, Iraq. Medics cut off his uniform in the field, and Thomas was stabilized and sent to the same center as Seargent Anderson. But he had no clothes. His physical therapist suggested he try the Red Cross. Dressed in a donated T-shirt and sweatpants, he was awarded the Purple Heart, sans underwear.

Many, many others come home with wounds visible or not, only to face daunting challenges in picking up their lives where they left off and trying to resume a normal life.

In contrast, when Bryan was released, he was flown to Chicago and greeted as a hero. "American Airlines greets him in the tarmac with hoses spraying arches of water, and cheering citizens line the roads that lead to his home town..."[28]

All this has not been lost on Bryan.

Everything that has happened to me since I've been hurt has happened to me because I've been hurt. I got to go to the Pentagon. There's this quarter-mile-long hallway that is just filled with people, and I mean filled with people. There's a little space to go through and everyone is clapping and crying and coming up and hugging you. Okay, that's great. But what about all the people who did the same exact thing that I did that didn't get hurt? They should get the same recognition we do. We all did the same thing.[29]

How Systems Can Set Up PTG

In a best-case scenario, the two partners of helper and patient in a comprehensive rehabilitation system would work in concert, complementing and enhancing each other's effectiveness. The natural limitations of time, money, and resources imposed on medical and rehabilitation systems can be used to full advantage when both partners clearly identify their boundaries, with thresholds beyond which only the rehabilitating person cum choice maker can step. Helpers can then set the stage for PTG by actively changing roles in the different phases of the Creation Cycle, with phases often activated simultaneously.

CRISIS PHASE

Helper Actions

Helpers provide direct care and resources to correct all problems within their scope of expertise and resources. They will:

- Take all possible action to save life and limb.
- Provide appropriate medical and psychological aid to prevent further damage.
- Provide resources to fix problems such as engaging insurance systems to rebuild home, replace loss, and pay medical costs.
- Lay out the road map for the Creation Cycle but not define an end point or put restrictions on possible outcomes. Statistics notwithstanding, any end points are basically conjectural and not dependent on the precrisis state or others' experiences.

Patient Actions

- Seek appropriate resources to resolve the problem.
- Observe what identities or attachments may be at stake.
- Feel the fear. Feel the loss.
- Allow expression of emotions that do not damage yourself or others.
- Avoid projecting problems on others. This is your experience.

CHAOS PHASE

Helper Actions

Helpers now make the shift from helper to coach, mapping out and supporting the elements of the Creation Cycle and the person's central role in it. They aim to:

- Identify a clear boundary marking the extent of the helper and institution's responsibilities and scope of services.
- Acknowledge the importance of the second element of chaos, *letting go to all possibilities.*
- Support grief and letting-go processes through coaching and counseling.
- Teach elements of the Creation Cycle and champion the person letting go to the power of chaos.
- Support patients in accepting themselves just as they are, thus allowing whole new opportunities and creations to blossom.

Patient Actions

- Let go ... let go!
- Express feelings as they arise, including pain, anger, shame. Find support as needed to help express and release emotions and past attachments.
- By choice, see opportunity. Experiment by taking new actions. Allow yourself to discover new ways of finding meaning.
- Follow your desires. Rekindle passions for connections. Reach out in new ways. Then let go of your expectations about the outcomes.
- Accept yourself as you are now.

CREATION PHASE

Helper Actions

Helpers remain in a coaching role, assisting the person throughout all phases to take responsibility for creative, ability-centered actions. As such they will:

- Support role reversal to ensure the patient, not the helping system, is in charge of possible outcomes and follow up with available resources and guidance.
- Maintain a clear edge defining the institution's responsibilities and the patient's choices.
- Champion the capacity for enhanced well-being and new opportunities as potential outcomes.
- Always envision the person as able to respond.

- Keep potential for healing open-ended, imposing no limits but empowering the individual's capacity for creating a quality life.

Patient Actions

- See yourself as responsible and able to act effectively, whatever the circumstances.

- Clarify desires. If the problems were fixed, what would you really want? Whatever the experiences sought—bring them to life now!

- Focus on taking actions that are aligned with current desires.

- Let go of expectations and possible results, and choose to see ability, worth, and creativity just now.

- Follow the mystery of unexpected possibilities. They open as you take action.

- Explore. Create new ways of expressing yourself. Seek new friends and contacts.

- Be flexible and willing to entertain paradox, conflicting perspectives, ambiguities. Let go of any expectations.

People who succeed in taking the reins of life again after crisis choose to take action toward what they desire, using resources and abilities they already possess. Their choices do not hinge on anything or anybody but themselves. They become choice makers and mapmakers of their own reality, allowing new ways of perceiving their world to lead themselves to expanded expressions of living.

Chapter 10
A Culture of Crisis

*We have to get people in touch with their essential self that
gives meaning, value, and purpose. Some people have to
experience trauma to make the necessary changes...
It's too bad we have to go through such deep pain to let go.*

— Gerald Levin, former CEO of Time Warner —

Even before we take our first breath, our worth is defined for us by the cultural contours of race, gender, and class. Each of us is birthed into a culture that (conveniently) tells who we are, what our role should be, how we differ from others born into other cultures. It tells us how to measure our importance, and it shapes our freedom—or lack thereof—to express our own innate desires.

It's true our cultural maps form an essential component of how we understand and communicate with one another. But we forget that "the map is not the territory," as they say. No map is entirely representative of the lay of the land, and a simple mis-reading can send us down an unfulfilling if not a well-worn path.

Graduating Money School

Here in the United States, of course, we can hardly escape early induction into the money culture. Throughout my youth, as I sought to understand the keys to successfully navigating the world around me, I learned that money is power... success... affluence... and influence. Money measures worth.

Everything could be compared and valued by stamping a monetary value on it.

In short, I saw that the more money we have, the happier we should be, and that the path of our lives should be aligned with working harder, being productive, and *getting there*. But a funny thing happened on the way to occupying my little cog in the wheel of endless productivity. A full array of the usual doubts, disappointments, and disillusionments of life visited me—and then some. Through some very pain-filled bumps along the road of life, I discovered, way down deep, I was unpersuaded that money was the answer.

Another View from the Top

Having arrived at a profoundly different bottom line from "Money is *It*," I'm not prepared to say money isn't a useful tool! Since, in our culture, the heads of corporations represent the pinnacle of achievement, power, and authority, I sought out some of these folks to test the premise of the Creation Cycle. Were they putting its principles into practice or reaping its benefits?

Gerald "Jerry" Levin, former CEO of Time Warner and architect of its $106-billion merger with AOL in 2000, had some answers for me.

Paradoxically, at the height of his influence and power, Jerry didn't know how to respond to the violent death of his own son in 1997, a schoolteacher who was robbed and murdered by one of his former students. At the time, Jerry coped with his grief and loss by working even harder. Only in retrospect, as he led his company through the turbulence wrought by the merger and events of 9/11, did he begin to understand the cost of his neglect.

A New Bell Was Tolling...

In an interview with Maria Bartiromo, anchor of CNBC's *Closing Bell*, Jerry revealed how growing through his loss and opening to insight brought profound changes to his life:

In the beginning it is difficult because there's a loud silence and everything seems to change. All the touch points of your identity have dissolved. That's the initial feeling. But then there's an exhilaration that comes from maybe establishing your true identity and finding your real purpose.

I think I'm the poster child for not paying attention to the most important thing in the world. The death of my son was probably the pivotal experience of my life. To not understand that, to not deal with it, to just return and work even harder—I hope people can understand and learn from that because I just put an iron curtain in front of my emotions. And our business culture actually encourages that: Your ability to negotiate and succeed comes not from being emotionally vulnerable; it comes from being almost a testosterone superman. What a terrible failing on my part not to have taken that tragedy and tried to understand.[30]

In 2006, Jerry told another reporter, Jim Goldman:

When 9/11 happened and I saw the faces of mothers, brothers, fathers, cousins, sisters, who had lost someone, who had simply gone to work, that brought up the pain in my own family. . . .

And then I had to stand up and give a Wall St. report and the first question was, "Are some of the activities that you're doing"—because we were trying to help out with a lot of the survivors—"how is that going to affect our margins in the next quarter?" And I literally lost it at one meeting . . . my responsibility was running head-long into this wave of emotion that I had no way of expressing."[31]

Goodbye, "Testosterone Superman"!

Jerry recounted to Goldman how something clicked in him.

> *At that point, it was easy to say goodbye. I didn't know where I was going, but I knew I was going on a journey, and I knew it had to be outside of the business world.* [32]

When asked what was now important to him, the once most powerful media executive in the world responded.

> *Family, love, having a sense of purpose, having something in the core, something in the center beyond money and power and recognition, because it's all fleeting.* [33]

By the time I spoke with Jerry in 2008, he had tasted life outside the circle of corporate power long enough to see how limited his former life had been, despite his wealth. I asked him to look back and reflect on the trajectory his life had taken over the eight years since his son's death. How had change come about?

He answered simply,

> *I was transported out of the environment of business to engage in more meaningful ways, much more fulfilling than anything I attained in the corporate realm … I went from an uncaring existential belief lost in résumés and the turmoil of the business world to find a deeper and much richer way of being. I see lessons and meaning in everything.*

Jerry neatly summed up the essential message choice makers have to offer us:

> *We need to get people in touch with their essential self that gives meaning, value, and purpose. Some people have to experience trauma to make the necessary changes. I think it's too bad we have to go through such deep pain to let go.*

Bill's Story

Bill English would agree. A successful business owner and executive in Salt Lake City, Bill was well-established financially and respected for his work in business, community, and country. He had received a Purple Heart after being wounded in Vietnam piloting a helicopter.

Driving in an off-road adventure one day, long after the war, Bill hit a hollow in the road. His jeep—and his world—flipped over. He landed upside down, his neck broken. In an instant, a life built up over decades of hard work literally collapsed.

Bill told me his last thoughts as he lost consciousness riveted not onto his business, his earnings, or his own demise. Nor on the long struggle to attain positions of leadership and power. What crowded out all other thoughts were images of his children, with whom he'd spent so little time while on the road to success. Feelings of desolation overtook him.

> *I had given my children everything, but with emphasis on every "thing." I had not really been present for them personally or emotionally.*

Emergency personnel soon arrived, keeping Bill alive until the expertise of emergency room doctors saved his life. He was in a coma for two months.

Although Bill is only partially recovered and will never walk again, he operates from a totally different mental map from the one that used to govern his actions and attitudes. Today he engages his life with vitality, humor, and compassion. And family.

He says,

> *If I see myself from the outside, I see a person in a chair limited, or I can see from the inside … I enjoy the challenge of creativity. I loved to cycle before the accident so I learned to hand cycle since I still have use of my upper body.*

Bill finds his life enriching, just the way it presents itself each day.

Not facing life fully is like nailing one foot on the floor. There is still movement, but you don't go anywhere except spin in circles.

You Can't Buy It

Perhaps you too learned about the ladder of success as a child. Didn't the big people ask you what you wanted to *be* when you grew up—doctor, lawyer, firefighter, policeman? All these occupations make the top of the list for societal prestige or bravery of service. So why then are suicide rates for these professions much *higher* than that for the general population?

No answers for us there.

Harvard psychologist Daniel Gilbert, in his book *Stumbling on Happiness*, examines the role of money and possessions in the pursuit of happiness. He concludes that except for those in abject poverty who lack the bare necessities to survive on a day-to-day basis, it doesn't really seem to matter how much money folks have. People in wealthy nations are about as happy as the Masai living in dung huts in Kenya. In fact, the Masai and other indigenous tribes around the world rate their happiness at the *same* level as the top four hundred richest people identified as the Forbes 400.[34]

Likewise, for answers as to what makes us happy, we can point to results from the longitudinal study at Harvard University that has been following the same cohort of promising male graduates since 1942 (among them John F. Kennedy). The study interviewed the men about their perceived well-being as they negotiated the usual passages of adulthood—career, marriage and family, retirement, and so on. The results? Looking back on their lives from the vantage of their sixties, these men cited their families as the number one source of satisfaction in their lives. Twenty years later, at age eighty-eight, those still alive said it was friends that made their lives worth living.

It seems that over time the fundamental things *do* apply.

Here and Now

Questions about which path might open the way to human fulfillment are hardly moot today, when there is widespread recognition that the foundations of the money culture could be under threat indefinitely. No one is forgetting just yet that the financial meltdown of 2008 brought the world to the brink of economic collapse, and so many of us have become reluctant stakeholders in the current national economy. Despite some of signs of recovery and a return to normalcy, doubts linger about where things might ultimately be headed.

Will we ever get our "normal" back? Do we really want it?

Meanwhile, despite the near occasion of "Great Depression 2.0" (U.S. Federal Reserve Chairman Ben Bernanke's nightmare term), our purchasing power remains dramatically greater than our grandparents could have imagined. We currently live in a fantasy world our ancestors could scarcely have envisioned—the true jet age—the era of laptops, cell phones, iPods, DVDs, second homes, freeways, cars with push-button everything, instant communication to everywhere.

Throw in cheap travel, low inflation, low interest rates, deregulated airfares taking us around the world, and still…we feel frustration and stress. Sometimes we'd just as soon toss out our ever-consuming cell phone, computer, TV, and refrigerator, and get off the grid. People managed somehow in the past to survive without all this stuff, and many of the world's people still do, right? But modern goods and services interweave themselves so tightly into the fabric of our daily lives, we wonder if we can really do it. Yesterday's dreams have become today's necessities.

We were an anxious, unhappy bunch even before the Big Bad Meltdown menaced our lives.

The fact is, we've been mourning the loss of the "good ol' days" and dreading a future looming dark upon the horizon for quite some time now.

When the Valley's Set in Stone

Our culture's path to "success" binds us in unspoken rules and mores before we even wet our first diaper. We grow into willing captives, unconsciously following deeply grooved channels of action and belief, much as a river courses in obedience to gravity betwixt sheer canyon walls.

We take on our cultural identifiers, defend them fiercely, then pass them on to future generations.

Along the way, if something we value is lost, or some belief to which we're fiercely attached comes under threat, we'll fight to defend our reality map. So too, a clan, a company, a community—even an entire culture—reacts to crisis not by looking deeper but by trying to throw off the problems that threaten existing values, identities, and relationships.

Community at War with Itself

For example, I live in a small community that has been at war with itself for several years. On one side are lined up those fighting for long-term economic survival through development, and on the other, the group defending the town's stability and integrity, grounded in its social fabric, artistic richness, and diversity.

Actions from one side invariably sparked rebuttals from the other—triggering predictable ongoing maneuvers and attacks and counterattacks. When I sat down separately with leaders of each side and carefully listened, I heard a detailed, well-articulated treatise of how the "other side" skewed and misinterpreted the facts. Those on each side defended their perspective as the only rational outcome to the problem, a dynamic that had fueled the ongoing attacks and counterattacks.

The scene went like this: Leaders from one side carefully laid out seventeen points defending their stance on development. Each point was logically supported by an impressive array of detailed facts. Having laid out their rationale completely, the group's spokesperson, shaking his head sadly, explained, "These are the facts—the other side has to be lying and cheating."

Carrying off this imposing list of "facts," I rather tentatively joined a meeting of the other side. There I was immediately confronted by an almost identical scene, but one played out from an entirely different perspective. After summing up their list of clear and logically supported facts, one leader confided, "There may be well-meaning people in the other group, but they *have* to be lying to come up with their conclusions."

The challenge was really about helping both sides come to understand that survival and quality of life must be two sides of the same coin—our life closely wraps around both. Each group was expressing one polarity of an unacknowledged, larger whole encompassing both sides' perspectives. However, if everything is seen from only one point of view, say heads, then the tails surely must lie.

Into the Land of Both/And

For a short time in this little hamlet, a willing minority from both sides who sincerely sought the best for the whole community came together to talk face to face. They experimented by disengaging from the content of their argument to observe how they put the argument itself together. In other words, they moved to step aside their respective reality maps. To do this, they employed the same simple process we've been discussing—making the shift from a problem-centered approach to a creative one. Simple, but not necessarily easy.

At a joint meeting, members of each side were asked what they would gain if they could eliminate all obstacles, roll over their opposition, and get exactly what they were fighting so hard for. What would be the result?

Each side quickly dug out their lists. However, rather than address them head-on, they introduced a new dynamic. Each side was invited to try on a victory stance: "If your side won, see yourself in the middle of your success. You just rolled over your opposition and have free reign. Then ask: 'What would I *experience* if my side won?'"

Silence.

Why were these dedicated people so unsure of the experiences they sought? Everyone knew the myriad problems confronting the town. They knew the people responsible for the problems. They could tell you in angry detail about who needed to change and what edifice needed erecting or demolishment, but nobody in the room—attorneys, architects, businesspeople, city councilmen, or citizens—could simply state the outcome of what they sought. One developer stated vaguely, "Growth is inevitable. We feel we are in the best position to direct it."

After some initial confusion about what the question meant, since they had spent recent years promoting or defending a particular point of view, a list quickly materialized from both sides.

Amazingly, each side came up with almost exactly the same list. A simple list, really. Without exception, everyone in the room was fighting for some very important values.

Their lists: safety, freedom, honoring diversity, individual right of expression, right to choose, a community of sharing and caring. Both sides perceived these basic needs as being threatened by the opposition and so naturally fought fiercely in their defense.

At one point, an attorney and an architect from opposing sides sat side by side. One turned to the other and said, "We've been fighting each other over how this community is to grow—but, what is 'growth' anyway? What does 'community' really mean?"

Us versus them suddenly became *we,* engendering a lively exploration of the intricate web woven by individuals and organizations into the complex tapestry of community. A door had finally cracked open to let in an entirely new conversation, leading to fresh questions and truly new ideas. This process was vastly more creative and productive than prospects for an unhappy compromise between two intractable polarities.

Based on the success of the meetings, the town leaders were encouraged by the group to implement a community-wide Visioning Project. It was doomed to failure from the start. Why? What wasn't addressed was the actual issue keeping people apart—both sides unknowingly tagging their core desires for healthy community to specific symbols of growth versus anti-growth.

And so the townspeople's perspectives remained glued to the past, as did the contours of the arguments for people's so-called vision. Since the larger community had not been involved in the evolution of perspective, its people predictably remained fixed in seeing only two opposing forces battling for center stage.

Without taking the time and effort to intentionally engage the Creation Cycle, several years later the town continued to battle itself as the two sides wound their way through the courts—each side holding fast—to the detriment of both survival and quality of life.

Ponder This!

Findings released in 2006 by researchers at Emory University shed a fascinating light on how we all cling to beliefs in face of inconvenient facts. Investigators took brain scans of staunch Democrats and Republicans while they read political statements from President George W. Bush and candidate John Kerry.

After reading *exactly* the same material, each side reached entirely *opposite* conclusions. Each participant would cherry-pick facts to support his or her own pre-existing beliefs. Both sides consistently denied obvious contradictions in their own stand but detected even slight discrepancies in the opposing side. What's more, brain scans revealed that no one, Republican or Democrat, showed what should have been increased activity in a brain normally engaged in reasoning. Instead, emotional areas of the brain lit up.

What did register on the scans was a dramatic increase in the circuits involving *reward*, a response similar to what addicts experience when they get a fix. "None of the circuits involved in conscious reasoning were particularly engaged," study spokesperson Dr. Drew Weston said. "We did not see any increased activation of the parts of the brain normally engaged during reasoning."[35]

It should be no big surprise, then, that study findings indicate that people can learn very little from new data in the face of strongly held beliefs.

New Meaning to "Political Junkies"

From these results, Dr. Weston concluded:

> *Essentially, it appears as if partisans twirl the cognitive kaleidoscope until they get the conclusions they want, and then they get massively reinforced for it … Everyone from executives and judges to scientists and politicians may reach emotionally biased judgments when they have a vested interest in how to interpret "the facts." The result is that partisan beliefs are calcified, and the person can learn very little from new data.* [36]

It seems that the more compelling the rational argument or emotional tug, the more people will fall into line and follow the herd, suppressing any creative response. Can anyone doubt that politicians, their handlers, and others wielding power and influence are paying close attention to such provocative findings?

Closer to home, notice that the oppositional strategies operating in my own small community resemble those reported in the Emory study. At whatever level these polarizing dynamics play out, however, it's the intense *attachment* to a belief that prevents more integrative responses from materializing, thus aborting the Creation Cycle and setting the stage for continued struggle.

These results bring to mind a certain type of caterpillar that follows the scent of other caterpillars crawling in front of it. Researchers would place the caterpillars on the rim of a vase, lining them up one behind the other around the entire rim circle. Next they placed a plant the caterpillars liked to eat in the middle of the vase, and watched what happened...

Missing the Good Stuff

Each caterpillar left a trail for the ones behind it to follow, and each follower picked up the trail. All the caterpillars marched and marched in a caterpillar parade as they circled the rim of the vase again and again. Around and around and around they went, each one following the scent of the one in front of it, marching along until they starved and died.

Dale Carnegie observed something similar as a boy growing up in the Midwest. He writes,

> I used to amuse myself by holding a stick across a gateway that the sheep had to pass through. After the first few sheep had jumped over the stick, I took it away; but all the other sheep leaped through the gateway over an imaginary barrier. The only reason for their jumping was that those in front had jumped. The sheep is not the only animal with that tendency. Almost all of us are prone to do what others are doing, to believe what others are believing, to accept, without question, the testimony of prominent people. [37]

If No One Sees It, Is It There?

One Internet site I ran across recently simply and elegantly demonstrated how we see only what we look for. A video shows a basketball game between one team dressed in white and the other in black. Viewers are asked to count how many passes the team in white makes before they shoot. Obeying blindly, so to speak, I could easily count thirteen passes before one of the players made a basket. I simply concentrated hard on the ball being tossed between white players darting through and around the black uniforms.

Meanwhile, I totally missed the person in a black bear costume dancing into and through both teams!

It seems we literally don't see what we're not looking for or expecting to see—especially if we have a stake in maintaining a particular point of view. Upton Sinclair put it succinctly: "It is difficult to get people to understand something when their salary depends upon them not understanding it."

Of Microcosm and Macrocosm

The Creation Cycle holds as true for cultures as for individuals—whole societies can stay stuck in crisis or conversely, move into higher orders of creation. Joseph Tainter, author of *The Collapse of Complex Societies,* examines in great detail what factors propel a society's collapse. One critical factor he identifies is the failure of a people or government to take action in the face of a catastrophic threat—for example, when facing destruction of their resource base or environmental degradation.[38]

To Tainter, this made no sense. Once the leaders of a complex society become aware that a resource base is deteriorating or their country was facing a serious crisis, the obvious course of action would be to take action. Responsible leaders should naturally strive to find ways to resolve the crisis before it overwhelms their society's capacity to even survive.

How could the leaders see a problem that threaten their country's very survival with no attempt at redress? Tainter wrote: "The alternative assumption—idleness in the face of disaster—requires a leap of faith at which we may rightly hesitate."

Jared Diamond takes the critique a step farther. He's written a fascinating account of how whole societies actually *choose* to self-destruct, titled *Collapse—How Societies Choose to Fail or Succeed*. In it, he examines numerous societies that have disappeared throughout history and what catalyzed their failure. These elements include hostile neighbors, friendly trade partners, and environmental damage resulting either from natural or human-made sources. According to Diamond, the key to collapse or survival is how a society chooses to respond to changing conditions and stresses.

The author identifies a number of ways societies fail to respond to threats to their very existence. These include failing to anticipate a problem before it occurs, perceiving a problem when it does emerge but explaining it away—or what Diamond calls "creeping normalcy," and resisting attempts to challenge current beliefs or practices of the culture. [39]

Note that all of these relate to the inability or unwillingness to set aside present belief systems to adopt new perspectives. As a result, no action is taken.

Holding to outmoded beliefs in the face of possible self-destruction seems ludicrous, but how many of us have acted like the captain who ignored the signs of danger and failed to turn the good ship *Titanic* toward a more rewarding path?

Expanding the Bottom Line—and Our Circle of Influence

Perhaps it's not just coincidence that the Library of Congress once identified two of the most influential books in American history to be the Bible and Ayn Rand's 1957 novel, *Atlas Shrugged*. While the Bible teaches man's need to transcend selfish interests for a higher purpose, Rand's vision is the celebration and triumph of a radically self-focused individualism. Her hero takes reason to be absolute and holds productive achievement as man's noblest activity. [40]

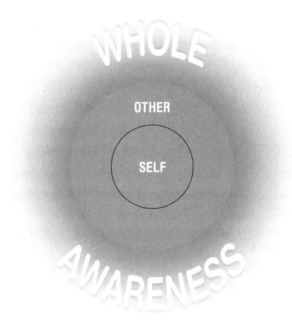

Figure 4. Expanding our Circle of Perception: Self, Other, Whole.

These two principles seem to be in opposition to each other, representing the age-old tension between the rights of individual expression versus the claims of the larger community. However, this is another false dichotomy. Figure 4 above illustrates how our expanding circles of reference fully and necessarily encompass both principles.

In other words, conscious choice makers increasingly enact both ethics simultaneously, expressing individual free choice while also choosing those activities and attitudes that directly contribute to the world about them. Using the Circle of Perception figure, observe whether your own choices serve the interests of yourself only or enhance the world around you. In any circumstance, you can ask yourself how your actions affect your own life and, inevitably, those in the greater community.

From awareness, we can choose perspectives simultaneously honoring self-interest and the interests of others. Notice that we can choose only those perspectives within our field of awareness.

Culture Shaped by You and Me

Emerson stated memorably, "Sow a thought and you reap an action; sow an act and you reap a habit; sow a habit and you reap a character; sow a character and you reap a destiny."

Self. Other. Whole. What we sow in our thoughts is the world we experience. We choose the perspective from which we identify and make all meaning.

We *are* both the river's water *and* the valley. And much more. Our personal choice and action carry the force of creativity like the power of sun and gravity and wind and rain to slowly transform the world around us. Each individual affects the whole, much as a pebble ripples and multiplies its effect within a river current, causing real changes downstream. The more expanded the sense of self, the more intentional growth results, positively influencing our relationships, families, and communities. Thus, expanding our Circle of Perception when we make our choices allows us full personal expression and freedom while enhancing the whole.

Tension between our individual rights versus well-being of the whole has existed from time immemorial. Rand reflects this tension in another of her books, *The Fountainhead:* "Why do they always teach us that it is easy and evil to do what we want and that we need discipline to restrain ourselves? It's the hardest thing in the world—to do what we want. And it takes the greatest kind of courage." [41]

Choice makers naturally let go to progressively larger circles of self-being, courageously aligned in their own expressions and desires of what they deeply want, while naturally contributing to the highest interests of the larger community within which they are embedded.

Old Men and the Sea

My next-door neighbor Bill fished for thirty years in Alaska's unforgiving Bering Sea, earning an enviable yearly catch in fish and dollars. Hard work and high profits attracted so many fishermen, however, that the government had to step in to control the fishery, effectively limiting his profit potential.

Today Bill, now in his eighties, owns a broader perspective than Bill the Fisherman competing against storms and other fishermen and overbearing government controls for his right to the biggest catch: "You know, if the government hadn't stepped in and regulated the fishing, we would have taken every fish out of the sea years ago. We had the technology. We had the fishing fleet and the competitive drive. But we all would have starved in the end."

In a sense, doesn't this describe the inner circle of serving only self-interest without regard to anyone else, ignoring or denying how one's actions affect others? In this case "other" means the generations to come, the descendents who would only read about the abundant salmon fisheries of their forefathers.

In the Pacific Northwest, the fight over diminishing salmon turns into a typical blame game. Commercial fishermen blame the Native Americans who fish by different rules under their treaty rights. The Natives point to the desecration of the land and the pollution poisoning vital spawning beds. Both groups rail against the damage to spawning grounds from huge dams generating hydroelectric power for the rapidly growing urban areas. Sport fishermen blame the commercial fishermen—both Native and non-Native—for overfishing.

All the fishermen complain about poor forest practices and poisons from agriculture and livestock wastes contaminating the rivers. And around it goes, fingers pointing, year after year.

At one point, a series of front-page articles in the *Seattle Times* exhaustively probed the problem. The investigators examined the impact and motivation of developers, sportsmen, utilities, foresters, Natives, municipalities, and government to determine where the problem really lay. Their final conclusion? It's all of us.

Feeding the Fish So They Feed Us

Many years later, the fight continues, but regulation has maintained at least a few sustainable fisheries in North America. I find my two boys flying out of school on the last day of spring classes to catch the summer salmon runs coming through the Bering Sea, one of the last viable fisheries on the Pacific Coast due to its remoteness.

They return carrying a couple months' accumulation of fish scales, whopper fish tales, and accounts of spending twenty-two hours fishing one day but only zero or two hours the next. Their idleness stemmed not from laziness or burnout but from the fact that the fishery closes when too few fish find their way into the river's mouth. Thus fishermen's freedom to cast their nets is inextricably woven into the web of the whole. The restrictions on fishing this year are balanced by having fish to catch next season.

Government control isn't necessary if fishermen take the long view and *self*-regulate, but this requires an expanded bottom line beyond just this year's personal profit margin.

Some call this the "triple bottom line"—expanding the Circle of Perception to include People, Profit, Planet. It's not just a Green-Age slogan. It works by effectively broadening our perceived circle of influence. When we as individuals identify ourselves as contributors to the well-being of interdependent and interconnected global communities, the inherent tension between individual rights versus others dissolves into a whole new discourse.

By expanding our circle of what we identify with, a new dynamic enters, one that moves everyone involved in the direction of inclusiveness and connection to the whole. The integrity of individual rights is fully honored in the expanded Circle of Perception, while each individual directly adds to the larger good.

At the Crossroads

Meanwhile, we do find ourselves at what seems to be a momentous crossroads in our global story, and necessarily our personal story as well—one where the past is beyond reclaiming but the future seems foreboding. Yet the conscious choice makers who appear in these pages point us in another direction altogether.

They help us to see that our attempts to attain fulfillment from external sources requires control and power over our circumstances and potential competitors, which in turn requires us to manipulate the world around us to a degree that's simply unsustainable.

Conscious choice makers show us how to bypass this whole dynamic, letting go to a wholeness and well-being already present within each of us. They tell us we can create a rich world from the inside *out*.

Will we listen?

Chapter 11
Beyond the Edge of Science

*The need for mystery is greater
than the need for answers.*

— Ken Kesey —

Once upon a time, a long, long time ago, our world was flat. And smack-dab in the center of the universe. These facts were so obvious, so blatantly true from people's everyday experience of watching the moon and stars circle about us, that their reality was deemed indisputable. Besides, the authorities decreed it was so and drew their maps accordingly.

Still, a few inspired people chose to observe the skies anew, coming up with a revolutionary notion about our cherished place in the galaxy. Their maps reflected a galaxy that flung the earth from the center into its outer reaches and made it whirl around like a top. Our history books tell us they were vilified and persecuted in an ultimately vain attempt to cling to a flat, earth-centric worldview. Old beliefs held sway for generations until people began to listen, and open to seeing the world in a startling new way.

Once upon a time, not so long ago, human bodies were merely a collection of atoms globbed together in an incredibly complex but ultimately predictable way. All actions were reducible to predictable processes determined by bio-physiological pathways. This fact, too, was obvious. Institutions evolved around this truth, and our authorities decreed it was so.

Then a few intrepid explorers began to experiment with other ways of perceiving the body. Some opened to the wisdom of healers grounded in ancient traditions, such as an exotic technique of relieving pain by sticking needles into the body. These wayward souls were laughed right out of the research laboratories and off the pages of the prestigious science journals. Still, more and more people began to listen, and question. Today, many millions of Americans and Europeans can even get insurance coverage for acupuncture, even though no scientist in the world can tell us why it really works.

Once upon a time, the very time we inhabit, the brain is believed to be the mind, our consciousness mapped out to be contained entirely within its gray folds. Thought can be shown to spring forth from electrochemical impulses within this most complex organic structure on earth—some say in the whole of the cosmos. No matter where we go or what we think, our currently accepted beliefs tell us we have an inner subjective world of feeling and thought and an outside world of a fixed reality. This said reality can be confirmed through objective, scientifically verifiable experimentation, assuring that the mysteries of consciousness will eventually be fully conquered.

Meanwhile, decades of astonishing scientific progress and startling new insights seem to call for a radically new perspective for understanding the source of our own consciousness.

Convince Us Otherwise!

So what is reality anyway? Over time the world has become round and spins about the sun; bodies respond and heal using subtle energies hidden from our present theories; and if we look closely, the mind can be shown to easily escape the boundaries of the brain, but only if we are willing to tear up the map and look anew.

No doubt about it, all these once-upon-time "truths" have shown great staying power. All *worked* because each held predictive power to tame the unknown and map out a framework for human understanding. The sun "rising" and "setting" is embedded in our very language, even though it's the earth spinning itself in and out of the sun's light that makes for day and night. A sun circling the earth fits our daily observations and works well—except for astronauts and a few wandering planets.

Like any dynamic system, the body of scientific beliefs evolves over time, and many scientists only grudgingly, if at all, adopt new explanatory paradigms. Geologists in the 1800s believed all features on the earth could be explained through gradual changes over time and that meteors had once impacted the earth only in its early history. In 1807, Thomas Jefferson was purported to echo these prevailing beliefs when he was told that two scientists from Yale claimed a meteorite had recently fallen from the skies in Weston, Connecticut. He reportedly retorted, "It is easier to believe that two Yankee professors would lie than that stones would fall from heaven." [42]

This statement seems uncharacteristic of Jefferson and his famous ability to forge new creations. Closer inquiry finds that no actual source to the above statement can been found. Letters written by Jefferson did reveal his doubts about the findings but he did *not* discard them outright. Rather, his statements reflect an entirely different stance, one demonstrating his capacity to stand apart from existing beliefs and observe without predisposition to seek the truth, whatever its form. In excerpts from a letter dated February 1808 to Daniel Salmon, Jefferson wrote about the meteor event: "[I]ts descent from the atmosphere would present so much difficulty as to require careful examination ..." [43]

It's clear Jefferson remained skeptical about the bizarre notion of rocks falling from the sky, but he did not deny the possibility to honor his pre-existing belief. Remaining open to discovering a new map, Jefferson reflected in his letter to Salmon: "[T]he actual fact however is the thing to be established." [44]

One hundred and fifty years later, some scientists still smirked at the fantasy of meteors striking earth in spite of overwhelming and very direct evidence of them doing so. Professor G. C. Amstutz, in his 1964 textbook on geology, doggedly stuck to his beliefs even as he condemned how the "myth of flying saucers and of meteor impact craters swept around the world and even affected the scientists." [45]

In today's world, acceptance of new perspectives and head-spinning theories still take a beating from attachment to existing beliefs, even with hard evidence about their validity at hand. Nevertheless, we *can* trust that even today's cutting-edge ideas will one day give way to wholly new maps of understanding.

Is Chaos Exempt?

A relatively new branch of science is mapping a clearer framework for understanding how choice makers are somehow able to wade into the messiness of the unknown without expectations and to create anew, armed with nothing but clear intent and action.

Chaos theory, along with other relatively new theories such as quantum physics, was birthed from small gaps and irregularities in what was once thought to be the final theory explaining the universe. Chaos theory came on the scene in the 1970s, transforming our understanding of living systems by examining how order emanates from seemingly random events. It provides a powerful tool to study how apparently unrelated events can coalesce into an interconnected whole that cannot be predicted or described by just examining its parts.

All complex systems, certainly including the behavior of us human beings, or the weather, the stock market, a river's eddy, or a heartbeat, can be better understood by peering through the lens of chaos theory rather than classical physics. The theory provides a clearer, richer picture of human behavior by taking into account the complexity and volatility inherent in our ever-changing world.

What's more, it illustrates how the power within chaos can transform systems from one level of complexity to a higher order, thus making chaos an essential component in the Creation Cycle.

However, regardless of the powerful lens that chaos theory gives us, what remains hidden is the essence of our capacity to choose, our in-the-moment ability to hold awareness transcendent to the maelstrom.

The Wonder of Wonder

As a child lying in the grass with my school buddies, gazing at the stars, I wondered about my origins, the purpose of life, and the vastness of the universe. What's beyond the stars? What is beyond that? And beyond that? How did I come to be? The answers, I reluctantly learned, lay far beyond my ability to capture in a word or belief or equation.

We lust for understanding and meaning. Once something is understood, it can be controlled and molded to our wishes. What can be controlled need not be feared. For many, the hope of scientific insight is to understand and thereby find sanctuary, ensuring survival or salvation. Chaos theory adds one more nail in the coffin of the dream that science may one day provide complete answers, predictability, or safety from the unknown.

Today's truths form the fodder of tomorrow's jokes. Measuring IQ as a way of defining the inscrutable complex of skills that is intelligence may someday seem as quaint as the past fad of X-raying feet for proper shoe size. Trying to define the essence of who we are by chemical composition, equations, or concepts may someday seem as ridiculous and futile as the priests of old debating how many angels can dance on the head of a pin.

Perhaps we humans would do better to get beyond our preoccupation with answers, to again stand in wonder before the magnificent mysteries of our existence.

Combating the Panic Just under Our Feet

It's those unknown aspects of life igniting the flames of fear that we try to tame. The philosopher Ernest Becker calls this angst "the panic just under our feet": Am I good enough? Am I doing it right? How can I assure my survival? What happens to me after my body dies? These waves of wonderings, of course, reverberate throughout our search for the fundamental truth of who we are—keeping us seeking answers to the secrets of the universe, the miracles that will eradicate disease and make us whole, smart, successful, immortal...

This is as much an issue in religion as in science, or in any strongly held perspective. The Emory study of people twisting the facts to match their entrenched political beliefs, regardless of the truth, pales in comparison to our fierce attachment to beliefs surrounding original cause or the origin of the universe. These touch too deeply on questions of ultimate purpose and meaning. Robert Jastrow, the astronomer who founded NASA's Goddard Institute for Space Studies, puts it this way:

> *Scientists cannot bear the thought of a natural phenomenon that cannot be explained. There is a kind of religion in science; it is the religion of a person who believes there is order and harmony in the Universe. Every event can be explained in a rational way as the product of some previous event; every effect must have its cause.* [46]

But explain we do. When confronted by an unexplainable phenomenon like sticking needles in the body to relieve pain, many scientists who felt secure in the safety of their explanatory models still stood their ground.

And, if something cannot be explained, it's just plain ignored. The bestselling book, *The Brain That Changes Itself*, elegantly addresses how the brain changes in response to our choosing new ways of perceiving and acting. The book reconfigures existing maps so neurologists can now understand how it is possible for me to be writing these words when I had such significant brain damage after my seizure in 1997.[47] But fascinatingly, the book deals with the problem of consciousness, the choice maker, by completely ignoring the subject—a common device readily observed in many modern psychological texts. The index doesn't even contain the word "consciousness" or "awareness" or "choice." It fails to address who or what it is that makes the choices resulting in changes to the organic brain.

Not to challenge the statement that the organic brain, however complex, actually has the capacity to change itself is to contradict proven axioms in philosophy, mathematics, and science.

Stepping Beyond the Map's Edge

The stories related in Chapter 7 ("Some Just Forget to Die") cry out for new maps to point more clearly toward what constitutes healing. Indeed, I have not recounted other patterns clearly observed in people transforming the quality of their lives through crisis, since no currently accepted scientific or cultural map can adequately explain the observations. But does that mean they are not real? Or, is it perhaps that our present models are not sufficient to encompass them?

The placebo effect certainly remains a mystery to present science. All manner of rationales are used to justify or gloss over this wrinkle in what otherwise appears to be a solid and sensible understanding of reality. But like the physics of Newton, which ironed out all but a niggling few little wrinkles in explaining the mysteries of the universe, the pesky placebo may one day morph into a portal that leads medicine to etch greatly expanded maps of how to perceive and bring forth health from the human body.

If we were to try to capture the totality of awareness within the Circle of Perception diagram from Chapter 5, we soon discover it is not possible. Maslow appeared to arrive at the same conclusion when late in his career he added the new level of Transcendence to his Hierarchy of Needs.

The response in the field of psychology to such a dramatic change in his model has been less than dramatic. This is in part because of the lack of wide access to some of his later writings; but it is also because the psychology field of his time was not "ready to incorporate Maslow's concept of self-transcendence into the quasi-official canon of acceptable theory." [48]

Even the word "wholeness" used in the outer ring of the diagram in Chapter 10 escapes complete understanding. How can we possibly contain the whole of a river's waters and rocks and forests and rains and winds and ocean and sun and beyond? The whole cannot be fully grasped by the mind, which vainly attempts to embrace the whole by caricature, model, or symbol.

Science confronts the same limitations in its quest for understanding nature's secrets. The power of the scientific method lies in its practitioners' ability to objectively observe and map the behavior of matter and energy, which requires a distinct separation between the observer and what is being observed.

What science is incapable of doing is turning around to fully capture the observer—and thus awareness itself (see Figure 5).

Take the expansiveness of love, for example. The inner box of concepts and beliefs can point indirectly to describe the qualities and felt emotions, even ferret out the biochemistry of love, but it cannot fully encompass the actual experience. Without awareness of our thoughts or actual experience, we lose the capacity for choice. We may find ourselves swept away by love's embrace, for instance, only belatedly realizing the foolishness of our actions.

Which perspective we adopt at a given moment colors every experience, what we think about it, and what actions seem appropriate. At any moment, we have the choice to expand our circle of awareness to embrace an infinite array of experiences and thoughts.

Figure 5. The Circle of Perception has no outer limit. The outer grey field represents every possible experience. The inner box represents our thoughts and beliefs about our experiences. The inner solid part of the grey field represents experience that can be defined and understood by anyone, like the color "grey." The outer grey gradually fades into nothingness and represents transcendent states, such as love or spiritual experiences of unity. Awareness forever escapes capture by any thought or experience.

To Educate—To Bring Forth

Trying to understand the whole is like a raindrop trying to understand the river the moment after splashing onto its surface. Masters of every religion as well as scientists reaching for fundamental truths all resort to metaphor and symbolism to convey what lies beyond our mind's ability to capture in concept.

Quantum physicist Erwin Schrödinger succinctly describes the dilemma of trying to grasp the whole from the level of egoic consciousness:

The reason why our ... thinking ego is met nowhere within our scientific world picture can easily be indicated in seven words: because it is itself that world picture. It is identical with the whole and therefore cannot be contained in it as part of it. [49]

Our ability to observe beyond the edges of current beliefs and scientific theories and religious dogmas opens a window into our vastness. If we can come to see this as a culture, we may truly realize the promise of education, as contained in its Latin root, *educar—to bring forth*—and let rise the wisdom latent within us. In the process, the differences and barriers we fight over today fade into utter negligibility.

By actively engaging the Creation Cycle from the perspective of being the observer *and* chooser of our perceptions, we can continually challenge present beliefs about who we are, our value, purpose, and relationship to the whole. By observation, we can see that the very foundations of what we call reality inevitably root themselves in comparisons the mind must make to create meaning. Each thought, then, becomes our tool to sculpt meaning—meaning totally dependent upon the perspective framing it.

By holding our concepts lightly and allowing our awareness to sweep past their edges, we can directly let go to expanded states of being uncircumcised by the boundaries of thought. We become like the river valley inseparable from its flowing waters, from the seas, from the sun and clouds and wind and sky… and still hold our precious gift of awareness outside it all.

Many of the people interviewed for this book talk about the transformative power of crisis as having been a "spiritual" experience more than anything else. If they do try to label it in some other way, they use many caveats. The implication clearly is that no psychological model, religious belief, or scientific theory can encompass the totality of what they experienced. Take Mark, for one example.

Mark

Like most of the people I interviewed, Mark looked upon the world with new eyes after his crisis, even though he didn't recognize the potency of the change until well afterward. Diagnosed with Hodgkin's lymphoma at the unusually young age of nineteen, he underwent an extraordinarily aggressive course of treatment. But this first round failed. When the doctor gave him the news, he remembers that his head dropped into his chest. He felt utterly defeated. For the first time in his life, Mark felt his mortality and a dread terror at the prospect of dying.

After enduring an equally aggressive second round, he likened it to shooting a bazooka at a mouse with the hope of killing the disease and not the mouse. Once complete, he found that he had not only survived, but the lymphoma was gone.

I talked with Mark many years later when our respective sons played high school soccer together. He related how in tough situations he would take a line from the 1970s movie *Deliverance*. When in an impossible situation with no way back or forward, one of the men would ask the others, "Well, what are we gonna do?"

They could lie down and die, or take a step in some direction, any direction. So, when stopped dead in his tracks by an insurmountable problem, Mark learned to pose the same question: "Well, Mark, what *are* you gonna do?"

During the half-time break, I asked what imprint the illness had made on his life. He pondered a moment, then related a story.

One day last summer when I woke up in the early morning, I noticed my curtain emitting an orange light from the sunrise. In order to open the curtain, I had to slide out of bed on my knees and reach as far as I could. I raised the shutter, and kneeling frozen in place, just stared.

I listened, transfixed.

> *The orange glow infused the sky as it climbed above the mountain range in the east, bathing all the farmland around my house in the most amazing light. Here I was on my knees, motionless.*
>
> *I felt overwhelmed by the sight. I know there is something. ...*

He struggled to wrap words around the experience, but to no avail. Neither scientific theories nor religious beliefs could contain the moment. After several minutes, he finally concluded,

> *Whatever you want to call it. The Force? Whatever. Without the illness, I never would have paid any attention.*

To embrace such presence, we need to honor the edges of our mind's limits in its ability to capture such transcendent experiences in the same way we honor the edge of a rocky cliff. Since we know everything doesn't end at the cliff's edge, we don't pretend the "beyond" doesn't exist. This seems to be one of the clearest lessons Gary's story has to impart to us.

From CEO to Dying Sage—Gary Holz

From the pinnacle of success and power as a research physicist, inventor, and owner of an aerospace company employing seventy workers, Gary Holz slowly slid into anguished disability as his multiple sclerosis (MS) progressed. Like so many at the top, he'd obtained his status at a tremendous cost to his own overall quality of life.

Once an imposing man standing six feet two inches tall, Gary found himself now an invalid confined to a wheelchair. By the time I met him, he had regained a sparkle in his eye. His silver-streaked hair framed clear blue eyes, a quiet, gentle voice, and an inviting smile.

Almost his every movement required the assistance of others. I had pitched in with several others to help transfer him from a convalescent center to an independent living facility. Under his own power, he wheeled himself out of the building into the bright sunlight, coasting the downward slope of the walkway to the waiting ambulance. I remember the helpless look in his eyes as three of us hoisted him and his wheelchair into the back of it.

Clearly still uncomfortable with having to rely on the mercy and muscles of those around him to assist with his every need, he had only his eyes and words to express his gratitude.

"Thank you, guys. Thank you."

I became friends with Gary, following his progress into a new career in the health field. After obtaining a master's degree in nutrition and a second doctorate in immunology, he started his own clinical practice. His past career as a physicist, the many patents he owned, and the company he once founded seemed like lifetimes ago.

One day, sharing coffee in his kitchen, I asked him, "What has MS been to your life?"

Without hesitation, he looked me straight at me, his blue eyes clear and intense. "MS was the best goddamn thing that ever happened to me!"

Here was a man, once at the peak of power, accomplished by all the measurements of success in our society, a man used to being in charge and having all the answers for others. Multiple sclerosis had destroyed a flourishing career. It had confined him to a wheelchair with prospects of his being on the planet for only a short time longer. And MS was the best thing that had ever happened to him?

Gary has since written a book, *Logic of the Heart: Secrets of Aboriginal Healing,* about how he came to terms with his illness, to step forth (or roll forth) into a new way of being and understanding that set the framework for the rest of his life:

I was forty-three years old and had two years to live. I received my death sentence with despair. By then, I was spending most of my time in a wheelchair, had almost no feeling in my body, was catheterized, and could barely lift my arms to feed myself. Even so, I knew I was not ready to die. There was still so much that I wanted to experience.

And so I grieved. I grieved for the loss of things large and small. Like wading in the ocean and feeling the gentle touch of the water on my toes. Like bouncing a grandchild upon my knee. Like making love. My desperation was deep and black, and I felt totally alone.

And then there occurred a series of what I would have called strange coincidences, except that I have since come to believe there are no coincidences. Seeking relief from the unrelenting depression, I stopped in at a local jazz club. Perhaps the music would take my mind off my problems. It was so crowded that I almost turned back, but somehow felt compelled to go in.

Precisely because it was so crowded, I ended up talking to a woman from Australia. She happened to be a naturopath. We happened to talk about alternative healing methods, especially those of the Australian aboriginal people. She happened to know some extraordinary healers in an aboriginal tribe in the Australian Outback. She happened to have the phone number of one, Ray Spears, who spent part of his time in Brisbane. She happened to give it to me.

That was strange enough, but even stranger is that I had a strong urge to call him. It was completely out of character for me, but I did it. I called Ray. I asked him if he could help me. And although, as I found later, he and other healers in his tribe did not normally work with outsiders, he agreed to work with me.

A week later, this man who had devoted his life to physics, to logic, to hard facts, cold facts, rolled his wheelchair onto a plane bound for Australia. My family thought I was insane. There was a part of me that thought I was insane. But another part of me was saying that this was my only chance. What did I have to lose?

At the end of a grueling eighteen-hour flight sitting upright in my wheelchair, I was met in Brisbane by Ray. He told me that he was taking me to a village in the Outback where I would be working directly with another healer, a woman named Rose, and that he would assist her. A seven-hour drive brought us to the village where I met Rose and began the work of healing. She told me that the aboriginal people do not run a clinic out of their village. They do not treat outsiders, but they had agreed to treat me. In fact she told me that I was the first outsider in over forty years with whom this tribe had shared their medicine.

Under Ray and Rose's care, I began working eight to ten hours a day with the fifty-thousand-year-old aboriginal system of emotional, spiritual, and physical healing. Within a short time, I experienced the first miracle—sensation began to return to my body! The following days were joyful. I first began moving parts of my body that had been paralyzed. Then I became able to stand and, with some support, to walk.

One day, as I reached the outhouse to change catheters, I grabbed my cane from the back of the wheelchair and proceeded to drag myself forward using the wall and the cane for support. The few steps inside were slow and cumbersome as I fumbled to keep my balance. With most of my weight against the wall, I began the process of taking care of my catheter. As I reached out to check the insertion point in my penis, I felt the touch of my hand seared through me with incredible warmth. It can't be! I thought. My mind must be tormenting me and playing tricks on me. I braced myself against the wall, allowed my cane to drop, and began to pull out the catheter tube. With every inch, I felt its removal from my body.

As the physical sensation of actually being able to feel something again continued to escalate, the impact of what was happening came flooding into my whole being. I felt filled with love, as if I were catching a glimpse of my life through God's eyes. I experienced clarity of understanding that I had never touched on before.

In a burst of insight, I realized that everything I had thought was important—the pursuit of money, success, material possessions—was meaningless and empty. All my life I spent in the absence of feeling. I'd been merely going through the motions and missing out on joy, sorrow, love, forgiveness, and compassion—the very cornerstones of life. And now I saw clearly that what really mattered was a simple human ability to feel.

I fell to my knees in the dirt of the outhouse floor. I felt laughter rising inside of me, and I knew what my life and my MS had been trying to teach me—that there is beauty and perfection to be found even in tragedy and pain. I thought I'd been playing the tune of my life all along, but all along I've been in the middle of a fully orchestrated symphony with a glorious conductor. The keyhole through which I glimpsed my life now became an open door. Everything was possible.

The moment when I began to regain the feeling in my body was the moment that I truly passed over the threshold from death to life. Although I had had powerful experiences working with Ray and Rose, nothing had shaken me to my core, made me truly consciously believe that I was really going to live, like the feeling of that catheter searing through my penis.

I had come full circle. The numbness in my penis was what finally convinced me to go to the doctor all those years ago. Now, the first part of me to live again, to feel alive again, was my manhood. I saw that as my past and present were being healed, my entire future was being re-written. I was not the man I had been when I first got off that plane in Brisbane. I was reborn.

With tears of joy in my cheeks, I started calling Ray.

"What happened?"

I handed him my catheter and told them that I could feel again. Ray's face lit up with joy. "Gary, you've done it! You're finally getting out of your head. What did I tell you? Was it a long trip?"

"It took a lifetime," I said, laughing and crying at the same time.

At that moment Ray shouted out what I can only describe as a chant of celebration in his own language. I don't know what he said, but everyone in the village came running. The whole group—men, women, and children—hurried toward us and began whooping with joy. They patted me on the back as they learned the news and, even though I didn't understand the language, I knew they were telling me how happy they were for me.

I was a man who had devoted his life to intellectual pursuits, following the logic of the head. What I found in the Outback was a system that could teach me how to know and trust the logic of the heart. It was a system that was strong enough and thorough enough to transform my entire way of looking at life, for it was really my belief system that was manifesting as MS in my body and literally killing me.[50]

Before his diagnosis of MS arrived to shock him awake, what Gary had lacked in his life was the experience of being open, sharing emotionally and working as an equal partner in relationships. He told me that for years he put in long hours at work but might speak only a dozen words to someone in an entire day that didn't relate somehow to his job.

The physical gains from his time spent with the aboriginal healers was not sustained once he returned home, but his well-being and quality of life continued to expand, regardless of his physical state. In the end, he arrived at a new relationship with life, embracing all of it—the good, the bad, and the ugly—including his impending death. His vibrancy, intelligence, and gentleness set him on a new course of helping others.

All this isn't to say his emotions didn't have their way at times. When I called him for one lunch date not long after he knew his body was disintegrating and he was sliding toward death, I suddenly felt on guard by the tone of his voice. I asked, "What's happening?"

"Depressed." His voice broke a little, and he rushed to change the subject. He finally told me he felt at a loss, knowing he was dying, but not knowing quite how to respond to the feelings welling up.

But by the day of our appointment, the sparkle was back.

"Emotions certainly do have their day," he admitted. "But that's about the extent of them. The sadness, tears, and fears don't get stuffed away like they used to…"

Now that his body was clearly deteriorating, I asked him again what effect the disease had stamped on his life, as we sat together in our favorite, wheelchair-accessible coffee shop.

He picked through his omelet for a moment, then said simply, "Equanimity."

Gary lived until 2007, fifteen years longer than expected. But if you asked him if he healed, he would answer with an emphatic "Yes!"

Chapter 12
Beyond the Edge of Life

Either everything is a miracle
or nothing is a miracle.

— Albert Einstein —

Just as a river springs from timeless mists and winds, only to be swept back into the ocean's expanse, we humans too will be called back into the unknown depths from which we sprang. Alas, we cannot conceive what lies beyond the dissolution of our bodies based on any direct experience, although material scientists confidently assure us it's the end of life, period.

But as we saw in the last chapter, science finds its roots in belief and interpretations of past events overlaid on the potentials of the future, always a step away from our actual in-the-moment experience.

Dead But Not Gone

In this regard, it's interesting to look at research findings concerning individuals whose cessation of brain or heart activity caused them to be pronounced clinically dead, but who were subsequently revived. These people often underwent dramatically altered perceptions of life very similar to those seen in our conscious choice makers who expand their circle of being to embrace a much richer appreciation of everyday life.

The December 15, 2001 issue of the prestigious medical journal *Lancet* features a thirteen-year study focused on patients who were clinically dead but later revived. Some patients claimed to have had a near-death experience (NDE). In the wake of their NDEs, these people found themselves more compassionate and less afraid of death as a final ending.

The author, Dutch cardiologist Pim van Lommel, concluded that no pattern in medical treatment is discernible among people who report an NDE. He found no correlation between any medical factors and NDEs among people who were determined clinically dead following a cardiac arrest and then successfully resuscitated. In such cases, the lack of blood flow to the brain typically results in flat electroencephalography readings, thus showing no electrical activity in the brain. If NDEs are a result of anoxia or other factors related to unconsciousness and lack of brain activity, then it should follow that all of the patients in the study would report an NDE, since they all were considered clinically dead. But Dr. van Lommel discovered that only 18 percent of the patients reported NDEs.

Dr. van Lommel observed a significant difference in those who did and did not report NDEs after being resuscitated after clinical death. The "life review" that people experience changes their values, and the subjects feel as if there is no difference between others and themselves:

> It's not about power, appearance, nice cars, clothes, a young body. It's about completely different things: love for yourself, for nature, for your fellow human beings. [51]

Scientists are finding intriguing hints of what might lie just beyond death's door and the final dissolution of the human body. Psychiatrist Bruce Greyson, director of the Division of Personality Studies at the University of Virginia, has studied the near-death phenomenon for the last twenty-five years. He concludes that whether NDEs are merely a product of a dying brain, as many scientists believe, or an example of a phenomenon that

requires modification of our current scientific models, as a growing number of others believe, depends upon the perspective tak-
en. Regardless, there is a dramatic change in people's lives and
values subsequent to their having an NDE.

An article published in 2007 in the *University of Virginia
Magazine* examined the ongoing scientific investigation of the
near-death experience. The author Lee Graves relates a story of
typical changes seen in the wake of an NDE, but from a very
untypical source:

> *Rocky collected money for the Mafia. A typical bagman,
> he was immersed in the material world of fast cars, quick
> cash and getting ahead by butting heads.*
>
> *One day, he was shot in the chest and left for dead on
> the street.*
>
> *He survived, though, and lived to tell of an experience
> that changed his life.*
>
> *"He described a blissful, typical near-death experience—
> seeing the light, communicating with a deity and seeing
> deceased relatives," says Bruce Greyson, a U. Va.-trained
> psychiatrist who interviewed Rocky after the shooting.*
>
> *"He came back with typical near-death aftereffects. He
> felt that cooperation and love were the important things,
> and that competition and material goods were irrelevant."*
>
> *That change in attitude didn't sit well with Rocky's
> Mafia friends, but they let him leave the family circle. It
> was his girlfriend who screamed bloody murder when he
> changed careers and started helping delinquent children
> and victims of spousal abuse.*
>
> *"She was just disgusted with him because, as she put it,
> he no longer cared for things of substance, meaning money
> and jewelry and fast cars. She couldn't believe what hap-
> pened to this guy," Greyson says.* [52]

Bill English, the Vietnam veteran and business executive who broke his neck in an off-road driving accident (See Chapter 10), highlights another type of adventure in consciousness not explicable in the current scientific paradigm. Bill has lectured about his experiences of being in a coma but having very vivid out-of-body experiences. Once he recovered consciousness, he was able to describe in accurate detail events that had happened around him while comatose.

He told me how one man in the audience responded to his talk at the University of Utah by dominating the question-and-answer session, asking question after question. "Afterwards," Bill recounted, "he came up and introduced himself to apologize for all the questions. It turned out he was a medical doctor who years before had a cardiac arrest which resulted in a near-death experience."

Beyond the River's End—NDE as Metaphor

As demonstrated in Rocky's story and hundreds of other NDE testimonies, the natural human impulse, once unleashed, seeks love and closer connection with others. Likewise, as we've seen throughout these pages, catastrophic crisis of any kind often results in the person expanding to new levels of well-being, surpassing even the precrisis state we call normal.

If the universe is intricately interconnected, as quantum theory suggests, and all religions point toward, then it seems plausible that we can, and do, share any and all experiences at some level. In both systems, all manifest phenomena, including human beings at their most fundamental physical levels, eventually merge into one another like separate rivers emptying into the ocean's vastness. Both perspectives suggest that separation of the observer from whomever or whatever is observed (subject versus object) finally merges into ... what?

Pure awareness, perhaps. Thus, both science and religion point toward an ultimate unity beyond separation. Einstein reached his own profound conclusion:

> *A human being is part of the whole, called by us "universe," a part limited in time and space. He experiences himself, his thoughts and feelings, as something separate from the rest—a kind of optical delusion of consciousness. This delusion is a kind of prison for us, restricting us to our personal desires and to affection for a few persons nearest to us. Our task must be to free ourselves from this prison by widening our circle of compassion to embrace all living creatures and the whole of nature in its beauty.* [53]

Calling Up My Own Experience

To approach this concept of unity, I want to share a small portion of a near-death experience that I experienced in 1997 as part of the grand mal seizure I recounted in Chapter 1. I was unconscious and barely breathing for approximately twenty minutes. It was the reason I felt so peaceful and serene when I awoke to firefighters crowding into my bedroom in the middle of the night and spiriting me away to the hospital.

Even today, I cannot cognitively grasp or interpret much of what I experienced, nor can any words possibly do it justice. It took many years to begin to integrate that event into what I now experience as a much-expanded relationship to the world around and within me. I include it here strictly as a metaphor, which requires no belief to have value to the reader.

> *While my wife watched in horror as her sleeping husband suddenly screamed beside her, then became unresponsive except for emitting a shallow, rattling death gasp, I journeyed beyond the edges of anything I could conceive to*

the most intense, most real, and by far the most expansive experience of my life.

I found myself floating but also seemingly moving, although there was no reference point to help indicate motion, direction, or speed. I felt weightless, even though I initially retained a sense of still being in my physical body. It was an incredible feeling, almost as if I had walked off the balcony of a tall building and suddenly discovered myself not falling to earth but floating in an infinite, weightless, and boundless expanse.

No reference point identified where I was, nor could my mind find any familiar "thing" to latch onto. At this point, I momentarily lost awareness or the sensation of being in a physical body but was very conscious of myself and my thoughts.

Soon, or eventually, since time became distorted, I began to make out that I wasn't entirely alone, or maybe a better way of describing it would be that the emptiness around me wasn't entirely empty. I gradually became aware of some substance—or rather some presence around me. Uncomfortably, I felt suspended, feeling surrounded by an indiscernible something, without form or identification but still palpable, whatever "it" was.

As I kept focusing on this presence in an otherwise empty void, I sensed a slight change. Slowly, the subtle presence surrounding me coalesced into what appeared as a small sphere of bright light directly in front of me. (The word "appeared" is used deliberately, since somehow I knew the light was infinite but had to take on a form my mind could perceive.) My mind finally could discern subtle differences between myself, light, and what was not light. I gazed uncomprehendingly at this appearance of light and a literal void surrounding it.

When the light coalesced more and more distinctly in front of me, my mind now had distinction and direction to help me orient myself. The light shone with a pure-white brilliance. Initially it seemed to hold no information, personality, or any "thing" my mind could grasp.

I again felt movement, sensing my body begin to approach or be drawn toward this light. Suddenly, memories of my life events began to well up, one by one, seemingly unbidden. It felt as if these events were attached to me by cords, and as the memory itself emerged into clarity at the other end of the cord, I could see the events clearly, not as memories but as if the events were being re-enacted for me, and I, the actor…

Once in the middle of re-enacting an event and experiencing its interwoven feelings, beliefs, and judgments, I was somehow presented the option of releasing attachment to it. When I came to peace with the experience, the cord and the memory dissolved, and the field of light grew brighter in front of me, exuding an essence of loving presence unnoticed before. Other memories spontaneously blossomed from nowhere, and the process of releasing them repeated. (It's interesting that in retrospect, I cannot remember the details of any of the particular life events shown to me.)

After each memory event dissolved, the light became brighter and brighter. The light now began to exude an incredible loving feeling.

One memory strand seemed particularly emotionally charged for me. I remember it concerned something for which I had sacrificed or suffered. I knew I had identified much of my life worth and value with this event, and as it began to dissolve in the increasing intensity of the light's loving presence, I shocked myself by rearing up and shouting, "I won't let that one go!"

As I shouted out, I wondered at how ludicrous it was that I was holding onto something so trivial amidst this overwhelmingly loving presence.

However, the attachment around which my core identity had glued itself was too strong for me to willingly release. Something would have to be surrendered of my own identification and value if I were to relinquish my attachment to what that memory represented to my life.

I do not remember letting go of this memory thread, but it finally seemed to dissipate on its own, still unresolved, as new cords revealed themselves, leading to other life experiences. This process of following memory cords to past events continued as I was drawn toward the edges of the light.

The light before me was infinite.

I knew that, yet, incongruously, it seemed also to be bounded, to have an edge. But trying to look outside its boundaries merely turned my brain into knots. I "saw" emptiness. Void. Nothing.

It wasn't like space emptiness as we know it from looking out into the vast universe surrounding earth—this space contains distance, time, movement, and relationship to objects within it. Space is what the universe hangs within. Rather, this was a pure void around the elongated ball of light. It contained no length, no depth, no time, no space, no dimension, nothing. No thing. The light contained the whole of the universe, and more.

The light now had clearly coalesced into a discrete elongated ball of loving luminescence in front of me. I suddenly realized the "substance" or ubiquitous presence I had felt earlier surrounding me was actually this ball of light. The difference was now I had a vantage point my mind could grasp. As the light became more and more distinctly formed, my mind could distinguish between what was me, what was the light, and what was not the light.

(Until I could distinguish separation between myself and the light, I felt much like the proverbial fish in the sea. The mind can only know through contrast and distinction. For instance, you and I are now traveling thousands of miles per hour around the sun without any experience of it, since our reference point for movement is our planet itself that is hurtling through space with us aboard.)

I wondered at this for some time. How can something be infinite, containing all that is, but apparently not seem to contain me? I still maintained a sense of "self" independent of the light.

My mind busily set out to encompass all of this until I noticed the light already filling my feet and lower legs. I now felt the presence of my physical body more strongly, which had faded during much of the life review process of releasing attachment to the life-event cords. But now I could feel and see my body, and watched as my lower legs began glowing in light, losing their familiar sensation of flesh and bone. Although the outline of my legs remained the same, they somehow did not belong fully to me anymore. Their form still discernible, they felt as if they were merging somehow into the infinite light in front of me.

The shape of the light also became more diffuse as I continued to merge with it, and I began to directly experience its vastness—an indescribable sense of unbounded Love, Presence, Being—but not coming from any particular direction or source. The light itself contained and embodied these qualities.

Feelings of ecstasy and loving bliss increased as the boundaries of my body and even my thoughts softened in their distinctness… and I felt myself slowly merge with this infinite, unconditionally loving presence. The pull to let go was indescribable—not commanding me in any way, but I was lured by a deep recognition of the light's essence and a nearly overwhelming desire to touch its universal love.

I continued to draw closer to and into the margin of the light's perceived edge, nothing propelling me but my intent and desire to experience the love emanating from its core. Waves of indescribable love washed over my mind and body.

Gradually, it dawned on me that if I were to let go… to fully merge with this miraculous presence of love enveloping me, the "Jim" I identified with would dissolve into the formlessness of the light itself. I hovered, suspended for some time half in and half out of it, feeling drawn toward the incredible love it radiated. Hesitating, I wondered if I could merge fully with it and still regain my identity and body, or whether I would die.

The light continued to fill my body, slowly turning my lower trunk into glowing luminescence. Suddenly, the realization struck that if I were to merge with this infinite loving consciousness, I would cease to exist along with my body. Who "I" was would disappear into boundless unity. I wrestled for some time with the question of how far I could merge into the light and not be totally assimilated or lost as a separate consciousness.

I withdrew my awareness from the universal presence slowly enveloping me to focus on "Jim" and felt the light withdraw without resistance. The boundary between me and the infinite presence before me became more distinct once more. Losing any fear of being taken over by the light's power, I once again drew near the edge to experience its intensity of love and unity and at least brush up against the experience of my own dissolution.

It felt as if I spent hours edging myself toward the point of no return, withdrawing slightly to regain a sense of self and my known boundaries of mind and body, and then allowing another merging into infinite oneness. I would focus on my individual consciousness in contrast to this absolute light of Ultimate Reality before me, feel the separation, and then allow myself to be drawn toward the light once more.

The light embodied the fulfillment and completion of everything I could ever possibly want. Yet, if merged with fully, my own identity as a separate entity in consciousness and form would melt into an eternity of timeless, spaceless unity. I would be letting go to true surrender, releasing all control, all volition, all capacity for choice.

Universal being. Pure potentiality. Oneness. No words could touch the power and breadth of the presence before me...

From my vantage I could see all dimensions of separation as illusionary—a creation. I struggled to retain both my identity as a separate consciousness yet somehow encompass as much as possible of this infinite presence gently enveloping me. Lingering on the edge of two domains, of forms and formless source, my mind tried in vain to grasp the unbounded state of unmanifest unity consciousness, and the domain of time and space and form—the essential ingredients of any creation.

How much could I fill myself with this powerful presence? Could I somehow bring this incredible unity back to my mind and body and my physical world? How much could I embrace of the light without disappearing into unbounded Presence?

> *After what seemed like hours on the threshold between unity and the illusion of separate manifest form, something unexpected happened. Much to my disappointment, I suddenly felt the light withdrawing from my body. It was as if some unseen dimmer switch slowly twirled the light into a gentle retreat. As the light continued to withdraw from my body, the realization took hold that I would be re-entering the physical life I had left behind. I felt the incredible experience of unity fading even as the light faded. The world composed of time and form, compared to the experience of undivided Being, seemed like so much papier-mâché and cardboard…*
>
> *I knew it could be no other way.*

Receive this account of my experience as you will. Words cannot possibly embrace its boundless expanse, but I know what I experienced. What I brought back from it is the conviction that the manifest universe of time and space we know requires polarity and differentiation—an illusion of separation. I say "illusion" because I knew emphatically that nothing can exist apart from the undifferentiated field of infinite unity and love and being I experienced.

What I can say is that to maintain a sense of self, to create, and to act, *some sort of separation in perception between the observer and the observed is required* to allow identity, volition, choice, and movement. All of creation can be seen as simply an out-picturing of apparent separation from the infinite. Time and space are constructs we require for playing in this phenomenal world we call reality, but they, too, ultimately dissolve into one indivisible source.

My NDE opened me to a state of being I know is possible for humans to attain without having to almost die. Einstein seemed to realize this himself when he stated: "The true value of a human being can be found in the degree to which he has found liberation from the self." [54]

That, in essence, is the message of this book. It is in letting go of our local truths and beliefs, our inflexible maps of what constitutes reality, that we step into vast possibilities beyond our wildest imaginations. It speaks to the power of choice. Being the observer and participant in this phenomenal world opens us to this miraculous adventure of Being Human.

Dare to let go. Your Self awaits.

Epilogue

As I neared the completion of this book, my neurologic and cardiac symptoms returned along with new challenges. After my second open-heart surgery in 2005 to replace the artificial valve implanted thirty years prior, I developed heart arrhythmias and congestive heart failure, a condition that limits my ability even to walk because of the erratic heartbeat.

A medical procedure helped to stabilize the heart rhythm temporarily, but my doctors state that nothing can be done to fix what they determine is irreversible congestive heart failure.

The neurologists' diagnosis of temporal lobe epilepsy with partial complex seizures has not responded to medication to date, and they remain uncontrolled, with ongoing symptoms that include significant memory loss, visual disturbances, and sensory changes that impede my ability to navigate through a day. I'm restricted from driving my car. Once placed on medical leave in May 2008, I focused all my energy on completing this book. Only one chapter was left to be completed, which I thought could be finished in a few weeks. Being off work allowed me to devote my days solely to the manuscript's completion. But many months later, the book remained a tangled mess, and would remain so today but for Joan Donovan's structural editing and her strict adherence to agreed timelines.

My own journey reveals to me life's possibility for richness and wonder untrammeled by circumstance. Although I am now unable to work in my career begun twenty-five years ago, every day presents an opportunity to choose to be constrained by my limitations or actively step into new possibilities. I am learning daily to more easily traverse the dark times shadowed by pain, sorrow, and fear, knowing it takes both the dark and the light to etch each other onto the very fabric of life.

Bibliography

CHAPTER 3. WHEN CHAOS BRINGS TRANSFORMATION

1. Janoff-Bulman, Ronnie, and I. H. Frieze. "A Theoretical Perspective for Understanding Reactions to Victimization." *Journal of Social Issues* 39, no. 2 (1983): 1–17.

2. Tedeschi, Richard G., Crystal L. Park, and Lawrence G. Calhoun, eds. *Posttraumatic Growth: Positive Changes in the Aftermath of Crisis.* Mahwah, New Jersey: Lawrence Erlbaum Associates, 1998.

3. Bauer, Jack, and George A. Bonanno. "I Can, I Do, I Am: The Narrative Differentiation of Self-Efficacy and Other Self-Evaluations while Adapting to Bereavement." *Journal of Research in Personality* 35, no. 4 (2001): 424–448.

CHAPTER 4. THE CREATION CYCLE

4. Inhelder, B., and J. Piaget. *The Growth of Logical Thinking from Childhood to Adolescence.* New York: Basic Books, 1958.

5. Borysenko, Joan. "Saying Yes to Change: The Anatomy of Spiritual Transformation." *Daily Word Magazine,* October 2007, http://www.unity.org/publications/archives/dailyWord/articles/sayingYesToChange.html (accessed March 2, 2010).

6. Ibid.

CHAPTER 5. WHO IS THE CHOOSER?

7. Gopnik, Alison, Andrew N. Meltzoff, and Patricia K. Kuhl. *The Scientist in the Crib: Minds, Brains, and How Children Learn.* New York: William Morrow and Company, 1999.

8. Frankl, Viktor E. *Man's Search for Meaning: An Introduction to Logotherapy.* New York: Washington Square Press, 1963.

9. Koltko-Rivera, Mark E. "Rediscovering the Later Version of Maslow's Hierarchy of Needs: Self-Transcendence and Opportunities for Theory, Research, and Unification." *Review of General Psychology* 10, no. 4 (2006): 305.

10. Ibid.

CHAPTER 6. SUPPORTING OTHERS

11.   Pierce, Christine. "Social Support as a Predictor of Post Traumatic Growth." Master's thesis, Eastern Washington University, 2003.

12.   Hill, George. "A Transformative Moment Sparks Change of Life." Produced by Nadia Reiman, *StoryCorps*, National Public Radio, February 22, 2008.

CHAPTER 7. SOME JUST FORGET TO DIE

13.   McDonald, Evelyn R., Sue A. Wiedenfeld, Al Hillel, Catherine Carpenter, and Rhoda A. Walter. "Survival in Amyotrophic Lateral Schlerosis: The Role of Psychological Factors." *Archives of Neurology* 51, no. 1 (January 1994): 17–23.

14.   Doidge, Norman. *The Brain That Changes Itself.* New York: Penguin Books, 2007.

15.   Tiller, William A., Walter E. Dibble, Jr., and Michael J. Kohane. *Conscious Acts of Creation: The Emergence of a New Physics.* Walnut Creek, California: Pavior Publishing, 2001.

16.   Crum, J. Alla, and Langer, Ellen. "Mind-Set Matters: Exercise and the Placebo Effect." *Psychological Science* 18, no. 2 (February 2007): 165–171.

17.   Uhlenhuth, E. H., Arthur Cantor, John O. Neustadt, and Henry E. Payson. "The Symptomatic Relief of Anxiety with Meprobamate, Phenobarbital and Placebo." *American Journal of Psychiatry* 115 (April 1959): 905–10.

18.   Katra, Jane, and Russell Targ. *The Heart of the Mind: How to Experience God Without Belief.* Novato, California: New Word Library, 1999.

19.   Frankl, Viktor E. *Man's Search for Meaning: An Introduction to Logotherapy.* New York: Washington Square Press, 1963.

CHAPTER 9. EMPOWERED HELPING SYSTEMS

20.   Taylor, Jill Bolte. *My Stroke of Insight: A Brain Scientist's Personal Journey.* New York: Penguin Group, 2009.

21.   Brenner, Paul. "The Five Stages of the Healer." *Journal of Holistic Health, Volume VII.* Mandala Holistic Health, 1982.

22.   Kübler-Ross, Elisabeth, and David Kessler. *Life Lessons: Two Experts on Death and Dying Teach Us About the Mysteries of Life and Living.* New York: Scribner, 2000.

23.   Ibid.

24.   Ibid.

25.   Kübler-Ross, Elisabeth, and David Kessler. *On Grief and Grieving: Finding the Meaning of Grief Through the Five Stages of Loss.* New York: Scribner, 2005.

26.   Ibid.

27.   Mockenhaupt, Brian. "What I've Learned: Bryan Anderson." *Esquire,* March 1, 2007.

28.   Hull, Anne, and Dana Priest. "Inside Mologne House, the Survivors of War Wrestle With Military Bureaucracy and Personal Demons." *The Washington Post,* February 19, 2007.

29.   Mockenhaupt, Brian. "What I've Learned: Bryan Anderson." *Esquire,* March 1, 2007.

CHAPTER 10. A CULTURE OF CRISIS

30.   Levin, Gerald. "Jerry Levin on What He's Learned in His Second Life." Interview by Maria Bartiromo, *BusinessWeek,* July 3, 2008, http://www.businessweek.com/magazine/content/08_28/b4092023838656.htm (accessed March 2, 2010).

31.   Levin, Gerald. "The New "Jerry" Levin." Interview by Jim Goldman, CNBC, December 19, 2006, http://www.cnbc.com/id/16269592 (accessed March 2, 2010).

32.   Ibid.

33.   Ibid.

34.   Gilbert, Daniel. *Stumbling on Happiness.* New York: Randomhouse, 2006.

35.   Westen, Drew. "Emory Study Lights Up the Political Brain." Paper presented at the annual conference of the Society for Personality and Social Psychology, Palm Springs, CA, January 28, 2006.

36.   Ibid.

37.   Carnegie, Dale. *Public Speaking and Influencing Men in Business.* Whitefish, Montana: Kessinger Publishing, 2003.

38.   Tainter, Joseph A. *The Collapse of Complex Societies.* Cambridge: Cambridge University Press, 1988.

39.   Diamond, Jared. *Collapse—How Societies Choose to Fail or Succeed.* New York: Viking Penguin, 2005.

40.   Rand, Ayn. *Atlas Shrugged.* New York: Plume, 1999.

41.   Rand, Ayn. *The Fountainhead.* New York: Plume, 1993.

CHAPTER 11. BEYOND THE EDGE OF SCIENCE

42. Milone, Eugene F., and William J. F. Wilson. *Solar System Astrophysics: Planetary Atmospheres and the Outer Solar System.* New York: Springer, 2008.

43. Ibid.

44. Ibid.

45. Amstutz, G. C. *Sedimentology and Ore Genesis.* Oxford: Elsevier, 1964.

46. Jastrow, Robert. *God and the Astronomers.* New York: W. W. Norton & Company, 2000.

47. Doidge, Norman. *The Brain That Changes Itself.* New York: Penguin Books, 2007.

48. Koltko-Rivera, Mark E. "Rediscovering the Later Version of Maslow's Hierarchy of Needs: Self-Transcendence and Opportunities for Theory, Research, and Unification." *Review of General Psychology* 10, no. 4 (2006): 305.

49. Schrödinger, Erwin. *Mind and Matter.* Cambridge: Cambridge University Press, 1958.

50. Holz, Gary. *Logic of the Heart: Secrets of Aboriginal Healing.* Place: Publisher forthcoming.

CHAPTER 12. BEYOND THE EDGE OF LIFE

51. Van Lommel, Pim. "Near-Death Experience in Survivors of Cardiac Arrest: A Prospective Study in the Netherlands." *Lancet* 358, no. 9298 (December 15, 2001): 2039–2045.

52. Graves, Lee. "Altered States: Scientists Analyze the Near-Death Experience." *The University of Virginia Magazine,* Summer 2007.

53. Einstein, Albert. Letter of 1950. "Einstein Urged Physicists Help Bar Arms Race." *The New York Times,* March 29, 1972.

54. Einstein, Albert. *Ideas and Opinions.* Based on Mein Weltbild, edited by Carl Seelig and other sources. Translated by Sonja Bargmann. New York: Three Rivers Press, 1995.

Permissions